The Program Management Office Advantage

The Program Management Office Advantage

A Powerful and Centralized Way for Organizations to Manage Projects

Lia Tjahjana, Paul Dwyer, and Mohsin Habib

HARPERCOLLINS
LEADERSHIP

AN IMPRINT OF HARPERCOLLINS

To our better halves:
David Roazen, Susan Dwyer, and Rahnuma Habib
With love and gratitude

Contents

Acknowledgments

When we first decided to write this book, we couldn't imagine how much support we would need from our families, friends, and colleagues.

We are forever grateful for your kindness.

First, we would like to thank our dear friend, Ikramul Wadud. Without him, the authors would have never met.

Second, we would like to thank our families and colleagues. We are forever indebted to our parents (Nata Tjahjana and Ginarthi Elpurba, Dr. Eamonn and Eileen Dwyer), who have engrained in us the value of hard work. Their advice and counsel helped us stay determined when things were challenging. A big thank-you goes out from Lia Tjahjana to siblings Rendy and Dea for their always positive words of encouragement. Paul Dwyer gives special thanks to his son Jack for reminding him what's important in life and to his colleagues Darren Pedroza and Chris Lopes, who were always there for him at project crunch time, even at three o'clock in the morning.

Third, we would like to thank our editors at AMACOM: Bob Shuman, who believed in us and gave us a chance to write this introductory book in the hope that it will benefit a lot of people; Bob Nirkind and Mike Sivilli, who were always supportive and gently guided us through the maze of the publishing business; and our copy editor, Fred Dahl, who was so patient with us and generous with his advice. To other staff in AMACOM who made this book possible, thank you, too.

Last but not least, we'd like to thank members of the project management community, whom we used freely to bounce off ideas and questions in search of perfection. We hope this book can provide some of the answers.

Boston
May 18, 2009

Introduction

For FAS Inc., a large financial advisory firm in downtown Boston, having hundreds of projects running at the same time is the norm. In other words, for CEO David Strassen and the senior project managers, Kerry Murphy and Bill Clements, having a headache is a part of their daily routine. As Bill puts it, "Every day, I have to play a game with my fellow project managers called 'beg for bodies.' In this game we meet and allocate our department staff to project teams. We use a spreadsheet to do this. The sheet tells us that we are overallocating everyone. It also tells us that even if they were available, we are out of budget. But still we play the game." They all feel that their projects are always restricted by cost, time, and available resources—ticking time bombs that can explode at any time. When failure is not an option, the pressure to successfully complete the projects takes its toll on some of the project managers.

Does the situation sound familiar to you? If yes, then a Program Management Office (PMO) might be the solution to your problem. This book introduces the concept of having a centralized office that manages the running of multiple projects at the same time and that has the aim of achieving an optimum performance for the whole organization. Throughout this book, we will draw examples from FAS Inc., which is based on a real-life company, so that we can learn from its experience in finding project solutions through the PMO.

Just like FAS Inc., to stay ahead of competitors in today's complex business environment, an organization must constantly respond to challenges. Organizations are always required to be both reactive and proactive to changes coming from the inside and outside, such as competitors' moves, changes in regulations, internal restructuring, and so on.

More often than not, responding to all of those challenges results in the running of multiple projects at any one time. The complexity of such a situation creates a number of issues, such as the following:

- *Scarcity of Resources.* Every organization, no matter how prosperous it is, has limited access to resources, be it human resources, financial funding, or time. With such limitations imposed on them, organizations must effectively allocate their resources among a number of different projects.

- *Inconsistency in the Management Process.* Inconsistency between one project and another is a common problem that plagues a lot of organizations, especially those whose project management capabilities are not yet mature. They are faced with difficulties in consistently measuring the performance of various projects. For example, Project A and Project B are two very similar projects with very similar outcomes. However, due to the lack of a PMO in the organization, these projects are managed differently with different performance metrics. As a result, Project A is deemed a failure and Project B a success, even though that may not be the case if a consistent measure were applied to both projects.

- *Lack of Coordination Between Projects.* With multiple projects running at once, a company is confronted with the difficulty of monitoring each project's success. It is important to be aware of how a lack of coordination will inevitably create disruptions in the organization. Examples are those projects that might have slipped "under the radar." While still costing the company money, they no longer deliver.

- *Difficulty of Selecting Projects That Are Aligned with the Organization's Vision and Mission.* Most organizations are confronted with this difficulty. Without a proper mechanism, irrelevant projects might be approved instead of those that are more valuable.

The running of multiple projects without the existence of a centralized coordinator will almost certainly result in a number of issues, such as these. Such problems interfere with the efficiency and effectiveness of an organization's business operation. As we all know, an organization that is not equipped to handle the challenges of today's competitive environment will soon lose its ability to survive in the market.

Objectives

The importance of having a proper project governance has been highlighted by a number of researches: A team from MIT Sloan Schools' Center for Information Systems Research found that "firms with superior IT [information technology] governance had more than 20% higher profits than firms with poor governance given the same strategic objectives" (Weill and Ross, 2004).

According to Gartner Research, the world's leading information technology research and advisory company, "IT organizations that establish enterprise standards for project management, including a project office with suitable governance, will experience half the major project cost overruns, delays, and cancellations of those that fail to do so" (Gartner Research, 2003).

In other words, Program Management Office (PMO)—also known as Project Center of Excellence, Project Management Group, and many other similar names—offers the solution. *The Program Management Office Advantage* introduces the PMO from a business perspective, as opposed to the narrow and more specific project perspective. Not only does it focus on the PMO's internal project-related activities (i.e., PMO's roles in monitoring projects' progress, implementing project management standards throughout the organization, selecting and auditing projects, and so on), it also discusses how the PMO will fit best into the organization (i.e., the justification to have a PMO, what needs to be taken into consideration before setting up the PMO, how to align the PMO with the organization's vision and mission, and so on). The concepts offered in this book can be used as a starting point for the readers to create the PMO that will serve their organizations best.

With emphasis on practicality, this book deliberately leaves out the complicated formulas and theoretical metrics associated with the technicalities of project management, which can be found in other, more advanced books.

In addition, the Project Management Institute's Project Management Body of Knowledge (PMBOK) and the UK Office of Government Commerce's PRINCE2—the de facto industry standards for project management theory—were referenced closely throughout the book as the main resource to base our overall PMO concept on.

Who Should Read This Book?

It is interesting to note that, although PMO is mainly pioneered (and widely used) in the IT industry, its practice is applicable to various industries, from construction to finance, from health care to education. The same goes for the concepts and ideas we offer here. Because of their generality, readers will easily be able to adopt most of them and adapt the rest to suit differing industries.

Regardless of the occupational field, however, we believe this will be of special interest to:

- Project managers who are already faced with the challenges of managing multiple projects at once

- Functional managers and company executives who are interested in improving the efficiency of the running of projects in their organizations

- General readers with an interest in project management and in the use of the Program Management Office (PMO)

How This Book Is Structured

The book is divided into five parts, paralleling the different aspects of a Program Management Office.

- The first part begins with a general overview of Program Management Office: key definitions used in the book, what a PMO does, the benefits of adopting a PMO, factors to consider before creating one, how a PMO relates to other parts of the organization, and so on.

- Assuming that by the end of the first part we are successful in convincing you of the useful purposes of a Program Management Office, the second part will discuss the PMO's role as a coordinator in detail. We outline all the major functions of a Program Management Office, from providing project management training to creating and implementing a standardized project management process.

- The third part discusses the systems and processes involved in the interaction between the PMO and the projects: for example, the processes involved in monitoring a program, the processes in selecting and auditing projects, and the processes in choosing the most suitable system to support the PMO.

- The fourth part looks at the Program Management Office as an independent business division. With sufficient understanding of the various aspects of a Program Management Office discussed in the preceding sections, the readers will then be introduced to the required steps in establishing and running a PMO. This includes preparing for the PMO (facilities wise, establishing governance, and envisioning the right type of leadership), implementing the PMO into the organization (i.e., dealing with resistance, which may be encountered), and measuring the PMO's performance through key performance indicators (KPIs) and audit processes.

◻ The fifth part consists of a brief chapter on the future direction or trend of the adoption of PMO across various industries. As organizations will continue to evolve, so will the PMOs morph their functions and roles to suit the organizations they serve. In this chapter, we discuss our vision of a future PMO and the journey to get there.

This book is structured in such a way that it can be a starting point for people to become familiar with Program Management Office. Not only does it provide the big picture of the concept, it also provides practical examples and templates that are general enough to be understood easily, yet detailed enough to provide guidance. We hope that, after reading the book, readers would be able to pinpoint how a PMO can improve their organization's performance and understand what steps are necessary to make it happen.

PART I

OVERVIEW

Defining the Program Management Office

In the Introduction, we highlighted how a modern-day organization is challenged to be constantly on the move and to be proactive against the changes in the business environment, as well as how such a situation prompts the organization to run multiple projects at any one time, each responding to a different challenge. We then briefly discussed how a Program Management Office (PMO) provides the solution, which allows the organization to be more efficient and effective in running the projects. Given that, this chapter provides a general overview of what a PMO does, what benefits a PMO offers, and the PMO's role in both the project and business environments.

However, before we begin, it is important to clearly define the meaning of the terms we'll use, because understandably there is still a lot of discussion on the blurred line that distinguishes project, program, and portfolio, thus impacting the terms "Program Management Office" and "Project Office." After reviewing the use of the terms by various organizations, definitions provided by governing bodies, and our own experience, we decided to adopt the following list.

Key Definitions

Project A structured process established to deliver specific outputs within the applicable constraints (time, cost, and quality) while taking into consideration elements such as risks and resources. Projects have a start date and an end date. In an organizational context, projects are created as means to respond to business changes, which may be a result of changes from outside the organization (e.g., a competitor's new strategy threatening the organization's market share, thus prompting an aggressive marketing project) or from inside the organization (e.g., key personnel leaving the organization, taking their knowledge with them, thus prompting a Knowledge Harvesting project [discussed in more detail in Chapter 8]).

Program A structured process of managing multiple ongoing projects within an organization. The focus of Program Management is the alignment of ongoing projects with the goals of the organization; thus the aim of a program is to group related projects that warrant optimum coordination of resources at the most beneficial allocation for the organization. In contrast to projects (which have a definite end date), programs tend to be ongoing.

Portfolio Simply a collection of programs. Portfolio management is about selecting a combination of programs that will give the organization the most optimized profits at the lowest risk. The Project Management Body of Knowledge (PMBOK) defines that the programs of the portfolio "may not necessarily be inter-dependant or directly related."

Project Office An administrative function of a project. A Project Office does not only provide key support to the project manager but also liaises with the Program Management Office to ensure that its project adopts the most current project management standards implemented by the PMO.

Program Management Office (PMO) An operation center that not only governs and supports projects from initiation to completion, but also plays an important role in improving an organization's project management capabilities. The ideal model for the PMO will greatly depend on the need of the organization and its ability to support it (discussed further in Chapter 3).

Note that although the terms "program management" and "port-folio management" are often used interchangeably, for consistency, we will adopt the term "Program Management Office" instead of "Portfolio Management Office" throughout the book. Our experience shows that the phrase "Program Management Office" is more commonly used, and we decided to adopt a term that most readers will be familiar with. Additionally, the term "portfolio" may create ambiguity within an organization because the same term is widely used in the finance department.

PMO in Project and Business Environments

Although the existence of a PMO is based largely on project management, its influence goes beyond the project environment. In this section, we will discuss the interactions involving the PMO in both the project and business environments.

In the *project environment*, the PMO is responsible for improving the organization's project management capability (see Figure 1.1). As the project authority, the PMO decides on the standard to be adhered to by all project participants. Its main role is to provide *centralized* monitoring and support for the projects and to bring them to successful completion. This means overseeing and liaising with the Project Offices (explained in more detail in the following chapters).

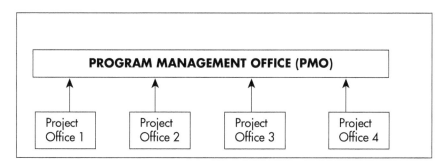

Figure 1.1 The Project Environment and its participants.

In the *business environment*, the PMO's role is to liaise between the business participants and the project participants (see Figure 1.2). For example, all business initiatives, once approved, will have to be implemented, in most cases, within a definite time period so that the impact can be immediate. At this stage, the PMO, in discussion with the business executives (i.e., the CEO, the CFO, or other departmental heads) will start the coordination with project staff to ensure that the business initiative is implemented within the allocated time, budget, and quality specifications.

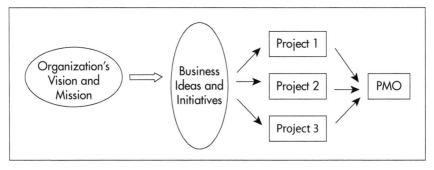

Figure 1.2 The Business Environment and its participants.

Benefits of a PMO

After reviewing the PMO's roles in both the project and business environments, we can see that the need for a Program Management Office is compounded by the following factors:

- Multiple projects result in competing demands for limited resources (people, space, infrastructure, and so on). Without the existence of a central organizer such as a Program Management Office, it is not easy to determine the best project for allocating resources.

- The degree of uncertainty from inside and outside the organization requires a flexible information flow to facilitate rapid and accurate communications among project participants.

- Interdependency among projects prompts centralized, high-level monitoring by a Program Management Office.

- Each project has its own management and administrative process, resulting in difficulties for an organization to measure the performance of one project against another.

- Lack of coordination among projects inevitably creates disruption in the day-to-day operation of the organization.

Program Management Office, as the central projects coordinator, has the main role in implementing a standardized project management process and procedure across the whole organization. Such standardization provides a solution to those problems, and it has a number of benefits to the organization, both projectwise and businesswise. Here are some examples of PMO benefits:

- It reduces the time and cost associated with setting up the project from scratch (thus avoiding "reinventing the wheel").

- It facilitates a faster response to changes imposed by a competitive business environment and improves the timeliness of projects' deliverables.

- It provides consistent means of measurement for all projects' performance.

- As the conduit between the projects and business executives, a PMO provides an efficient channel for the escalation (thus the resolution) of project issues, and it helps make project risks visible.

- PMO assists business executives by providing a high-level view of projects (strategic alignment, benefits, and performance), thus assisting them in making decisions on resource allocation.

- It manages project interdependency by acting as the communication hub for the projects.

- The PMO provides consistent project management training, reducing the need to outsource to external consultants.

- As projects come and go, the Program Management Office facilitates the formal retention of knowledge.

- The PMO can group related projects into programs to make possible the efficient use of resources.

- It ensures that programs are executed in such a way as to adhere to company goals and objectives.

- The PMO facilitates each program by the provision of tools and resources to assist the management teams.

- It provides management reporting to alert teams of project status and potential issues.

- It furnishes risk mitigation assistance when the risk is identified.

- It improves overall business performance.

These examples offer a glimpse of how a PMO offers benefits that every organization must weigh. However, as will be discussed in the following chapters, an organization must first have a clear understanding of what it will require from the PMO. Afterward, it can justify its decision and obtain the support of project participants.

PMO Activities

Although PMOs vary from one organization to another, the activities performed are generally the same. Here are some of those activities, which will be discussed in more detail in subsequent chapters:

- *Project Resource Management.* The PMO is responsible for coordinating resources (human resources, equipment, space, and so on) according to what each project demands and the amount of resources available (either from within the organization, from temporary resources, or through outsourcing).

- *Financial Management.* The PMO is required to produce a consolidated financial statement, compiled from each project, with a certain frequency (which could be weekly, monthly, quarterly, and/or yearly). The statement should contain information such as the actual budget and expenditure, as well as the projected budget and expenditure. In addition to monitoring the projects' progress, the information can also be used to determine funding allocation.

- *Vendor Management.* The PMO assists each Project Office with the management of third-party contracts with vendors.

- *Process Management.* The PMO standardizes and continuously improves the operational processes and procedures in the project environment.

- *Program Monitoring (Quality Management).* The PMO is responsible for monitoring the progress of each project in terms of schedule, scope, changes, cost, and quality. This is done through a gated approval process (discussed further in Chapter 12), the auditing process, and regular reporting to the PMO by each Project Office.

- *Project Selection.* The PMO assists the business executives with selecting projects that are aligned with the business by, among other things, identifying potential risks, reviewing the company's capabilities to undertake the projects, and the like.

- *Knowledge Management.* Knowledge management goes beyond managing data and documents. It also makes sure that all the knowledge gained and the lessons learned are not lost (i.e., by creating a project knowledge repository) when experienced personnel leave the company. More importantly, knowledge management is about making sure that the organization cultivates its existing project knowledge, continuously improving it and sharing it as a part of the staff development process.

◻ *Communications Management.* The PMO develops and implements a communication plan that involves all the stakeholders (e.g., the Project Offices and the business executives and steering committees). The activities may include the dissemination of information, escalation of issues, and others.

◻ *Customer Management.* The PMO's customers are those working both in the project environment and in the business environment. To maintain customer satisfaction, the PMO needs to engage its staff in continuous service improvement activities (such as customer service training, launching a survey on customers' satisfaction, and so on).

◻ *Training Management.* A proper training program is essential to the success of the PMO. It will enhance the skill sets of employees, train them in best practices, build expertise, and ultimately enhance the organization's ability to execute. It is the PMO's role to work closely with various Project Offices as well as with the organization's human resource coordinator to create a training program that is consistent with the organization's strategic positioning.

Conclusion

Now that we have presented our case on the need for PMO, readers should realize that having a PMO in the organization is not a one-size-fits-all approach. In the following chapter, we will discuss how the shape of the PMO will largely depend on the organization's need and capability to support it. We will also look at what measures can be used to justify a PMO.

5 Things You Need to Remember from This Chapter

1. The definitions of project, program, portfolio, Project Office, and Program Management Office

2. The importance of PMO's liaison between the project and business environments

3. Issues that prompt the need for PMO for an organization to maintain its competitive advantage

4. The benefits offered by PMO to an organization

5. The various activities carried out by the PMO

Justifying the Program Management Office

In the previous chapter, we discussed the abundant benefits offered by the PMO. It is no surprise, then, that the use of PMO as an integral part of an organization's success story is getting more and more common in large organizations such as Hewlett Packard, Bank of America, Morgan Stanley, and the U.S. Environmental Protection Agency (EPA), among many others. However, understandably, the establishment of a PMO requires a lot of investment, be it time, human resources, or money. Furthermore, the implementation of a PMO will result in big changes, such as changes to the organization's culture, structure, financial condition, and so on (discussed in the following chapters).

Because of the large impact a PMO has on an organization, it is important to realize and agree early on that the decision to set up a PMO should be a well thought-out business decision justified by the amount of return. Note that other important aspects have to be considered. For example, the PMO's capability level (i.e., its roles and authority) largely depends on the organization's needs and on the PMO's position in the organization's hierarchy, which is determined based on the most efficient interaction between the PMO and the rest of the organization. Given that, the decision-making process should go beyond the scope of monetary considerations.

This chapter looks at the various aspects to consider before justifying the need to establish a PMO in the organization. It also presents a viable method, the Cost-Benefit Analysis method, which attempts to quantify the cost and benefits related to the PMO, to help with the justification process.

Factors to Consider Before Establishing a PMO

It is essential for the success of a new PMO that there be a clear understanding beforehand of what will be required from the PMO, as well as whether the investment to achieve those capabilities will benefit the organization. Answers to the following questions indicate the organization's capacity and capability to incorporate a PMO into their structure.

Does the PMO fulfill the organization's needs? This is the most important question to answer in justifying a Program Management Office. Typically, the larger the organization, the greater the need is for a PMO. Large organizations are expected to have multiple projects running simultaneously, and each project can have fairly complex tasks with widely ranging impacts. In those circumstances, the justification for having a PMO can be straightforward because the impacts of losing control over multiple projects is often more expensive than the investment required to establish and implement a PMO.

Does the PMO fit the organization's goals? Generally speaking, the underlying idea for any company is to develop competitive advantages in the existing industry vis-à-vis its competitors. These competitive advantages are manifested through projects. For example, realizing that there is still a gap in the market for a certain product, a company may decide to launch a product development project to capture the market share. This makes projects a critical part in achieving the goals of an organization. Because the primary purpose of a PMO is to support the organization's strategies in achieving its vision and mission, there has to be a good fit between the company's plans and the PMO. Understanding the organization's aims impacts how the PMO will be introduced to the organization and how it will operate because it determines a number of things, such as:

- The appropriate level of capability and authority to allow the PMO to be most effective

- Whether the establishment of a PMO provides a suitable return on investment (ROI)

- How the PMO will make the organization more competitive

- The best place to position the PMO within the organizational chart

- How large the organization is—how big the PMO needs to be

- And so on

Is the organization mature enough to handle the change? What is the organization's culture, and how will it react to the PMO? An extremely important factor to consider when deciding to set up a PMO is the organization's culture and maturity. Culture can be a facilitator or a constraint. Just like every change that occurs in any organization, the creation of a PMO will face resistance from some people. Resistance could come from the (internal) project managers themselves, clients, vendors (external), or other stakeholders. Project managers may feel unnecessarily supervised by the PMO and hence resist such an authority, or they may simply try to protect their independence or avoid, in their opinion, more bureaucracies. It is incumbent on the top managers and the key managers to be the champions of the PMO and provide the support to make the change.

(More in-depth discussion on implementing a PMO is presented in Chapter 17.)

Does the organization have the capability to establish and run the PMO? Another important issue is the ability of the organization to equip the PMO with the required resources (financial resources, skilled staff, office space, time, equipment, sufficient project management competencies, business skills, and so on). It may be that the organization already has the capabilities and resources at its disposal and that they only need to get organized. Or it could be that the organization doesn't have the resources, in which case it will have to figure out ways to procure them. Although resource constraint is an immediate issue for most companies, it should not be a primary factor for considering a PMO.

What will be required from the PMO? Taking into consideration the organization's business strategic position, the decision makers need to define the PMO's goals/objectives, roles/functions, responsibilities, and authority. Having these items stated clearly ensures that the PMO can operate smoothly.

How will the PMO fit into the organization? The fit between the PMO and the organization's structure, culture, and operational processes is crucial if the PMO is to succeed. In terms of the PMO's role in the organization, the decision makers need to consider whether it is mainly a support function or a primary function, and whether it should be treated as a profit center or a cost center. As for the authority and reporting relationships, they need to weigh various factors before deciding where the PMO should be placed in the organization's hierarchy. A good balance must be struck between autonomy and dependence to optimize the PMO's performance. (More in-depth discussion of positioning the PMO within the organization's structure is presented in the next chapter.)

What will the PMO require to operate? What will its strategic positioning be? There is a wide range of factors to consider in answering this question. To be able to determine them, the decision makers need to consider both the internal and external environment of the organization. A number of factors from within the organization may affect the PMO's strategy and operation, such as the organization's geographic spread, the organization's value chain, and so on. There are also factors from outside the organization to consider, such as the competitors' position; market maturity; any political, legal, or social issues that may be prevalent in the PMO; and so on.

These questions are indicative of which direction an organization should take in preparing itself for a PMO. The readers are encouraged to think outside the box and be creative when questioning their own organizations' readiness for a PMO.

Justification Method

Upon answering those provocative questions, if an organization decides to establish a PMO, it needs to justify its decision. One of the methods that can be applied to make the judgment is *Cost-Benefit Analysis*. Since a detailed explanation of Cost-Benefit Analysis can be found in numerous finance textbooks, we will provide only an overview of the method.

Cost-Benefit Analysis

Cost-Benefit Analysis is a method to appraise the monetary value of a proposal by weighing the total expected benefits, both tangible and intangible, against the total expected costs, both tangible and intangible. However, the problem associated with such a method is quantifying a cost or benefit whose value is not readily available. For example, it will be easy to determine how much staffing the PMO will cost (estimated man-hours, estimated dollars per hour), but it will be difficult to forecast how much money the company will save in the future by adopting the PMO. At the end of the day, this method is still an estimate, with all the inaccuracies that come with it.

In the analysis, *cost* can be determined by allocating monetary

Making a Case: Justifying the PMO

CEO David Strassen of FAS Inc. had seen his company grow ten-fold in the last five years. As a result of increased regulatory scrutiny on finance companies, the systems solutions and consulting services his company offered specifically to assist those clients impacted by changes to the financial accounting standard had been very popular. However, lately, as his organization was managing more and more projects, the clients were complaining that they were not getting the service levels they agreed to. Dave's director of sales, James Holland, was accusing the technical team of not knowing what they're doing.

The technical team, who seemed to lack morale, was constantly delivering late and over budget. The product rollouts always seemed to have missed major requirements. When discovered, the misses were hastily fixed by the development teams without management review, and this had led to unexplainable cost overruns. Many of the programmers complained to the systems manager, Bill Clements, of stress and were often heard saying that they had too many poorly defined projects to work on at one time, leading to mistakes and poor product releases. Bill brought this to sales's James Holland, but the response he usually got was. "The customers are the reason we have a job." Bill complained to Dave that the sales team constantly "sells stuff we don't do or can't do." His budget had been exceeded by $300,000 last quarter alone. And he had just lost two of his best project managers, who no longer could stand the work pressure. "We have to come up with a solution, Dave," said Bill. Both Dave and Bill came across a PMO in an article in a project management magazine a while ago, and they thought this might be the solution to their problem.

Prompted by these problems and a constant headache from the people complaining to him, Dave decided to have Mackenzie & Co., a management consulting firm, come in and see what could be done to address some of the issues. After spending time on-site, Mackenzie suggested that the problems were not necessarily with his people, but with the processes they used, or the lack thereof. The firm determined that the company's activities could be split into three separate areas: expense reporting, international taxation, and specialty consulting. They recommended that Dave set up a program for each area and introduce a Program Management Office to run them. He liked the recommendations but knew he was not the person to carry them out. So he hired Paul Witten, a well-known program manager, to get the Office off the ground. (To be continued in the next chapters.)

---

values on the resources required to establish and run the PMO. These costs should be comprehensive and include those that are direct as well as indirect (e.g., travel cost, personnel cost, resource acquisition cost, and so on). Other types of costs, such as those to be discussed in this chapter, must also be considered.

Measuring opportunity cost (i.e., possible loss of profits due to the company's decision to invest in establishing and running the PMO instead of pursuing other opportunities) is always difficult and is usually an estimate. However, to get a full picture of the total costs associated with the PMO, the opportunity costs must be included (this includes both short-term and long-term costs). Recurring costs (i.e., regular cost such as electricity bills, staff salary, stationery purchases, and so on) and nonrecurring, one-time investment-type costs (e.g., investment to purchase equipment or fixed properties that rarely occur more than once due to their long life span) are other types of costs to be taken into account.

Benefits are positive outcomes that can be reasonably identified as the results of having a PMO in the organization (e.g., projects are run more efficiently resulting in cost savings, projects are selected more effectively yielding higher return to the company, and so on). Monetary values can easily be assigned to some outcomes, but others may be more difficult to value. In such instances, it may be useful to refer to the historical data and to conduct analysis on the amount of monetary loss in the past caused by the lack of projects' monitoring, analysis on the number of projects completed within schedule in the past, how much improvement can be achieved with a PMO, and so on.

Similar to costs, both real (or actual) and potential benefits should be assessed. Recurring and nonrecurring benefits must also be captured to the extent possible.

Example of Cost-Benefit Analysis: PMO Justification

Cost-Benefit Analysis typically adopts the time value of money. Bear in mind the financial concept of *discounted value*—the value of $1 in the future will be less than the value of $1 today due to inflation. Thus, monetary benefits that will occur in the future (note that the benefits from PMO are not always immediate) will have to be brought to today's value by using a discount rate. However, for the purpose of simplicity, the following example assumes that everything happens at time 0 (i.e., today, when all future values would have been discounted).

Benefits

1. Yearly savings from approving the "wrong" projects $300,000

2. Increased revenue from having a standardized
   project management process $190,000

3. Yearly savings from project costs that can be
   avoided by having a PMO $80,000

4. Increased revenue from improving staff's project
   management skills $50,000

Costs

1. Yearly PMO staff's salaries $350,000

2. Yearly equipment and space rental and purchase $50,000

3. Yearly PMO training $50,000

Assuming that all of the benefits and costs occur at time 0, the net income for the organization is $620,000 – $450,000 = $170,000 (increase of revenue per year). This scenario justifies establishing a PMO.

Conclusion

In this chapter, we have discussed the importance of justifying the establishment of a PMO. The next step, as will be discussed in the following chapter, is figuring out the PMO's level of capability and how exactly it should fit into the organization's structure.

5 Things You Need to Remember from This Chapter

1. How the presence of a PMO will greatly benefit an organization, and why it must be a justified business decision

2. The importance of knowing beforehand what the organization wants to get out of the PMO

3. How critical the issue of fit is to the success of the PMO, which has to suit the organization's culture, vision, and mission

4. The dependence of the PMO's capability level on what the organization can do to support it

5. An understanding of how to use the Cost-Benefit Analysis method, while realizing that it has its own strengths and weaknesses

The Program Management Office in the Organization

As we mentioned in the previous chapter, the justification for a PMO should be a well thought-out business decision. Once the organization decides that it needs a PMO, the next step is to consider the kind of PMO that will suit it best. To help answer that question, the organization must consider these two important aspects:

1. *The PMO's Capability Level.* What types of roles does the organization want it to carry out? What kind of authority, if any, should it have? Does the organization have the resources—time, money, people—to support the type of PMO it envisions?

2. *The PMO's Position in the Organization's Structure.* Where is the best place to locate the PMO so that its interaction with the rest of the organization is optimized?

This chapter will guide the readers to find the answers.

PMO and the Organization's Structure

The introduction of a PMO will likely have an effect on the organization's staffing structure because it could result in a shift of authority and resources within the organization. Before we look at where a PMO will best fit, we will first look at the common organization structures. The Project Management Body of Knowledge (PMBOK) has broken this down into three types: *functional, projectized,* and *matrixed.*

The Functional Organization

A functional organization is hierarchical, and the entire company is classified according to the specific functions performed (e.g., sales and marketing, accounting, human resources, finance, and so on). See Figure 3.1. In this structure, projects are undertaken on a departmental level. If multiple departments are involved, each is responsible for their own department-related tasks (i.e., the finance department will be concerned only with the financial aspect of the project, the human resources department will be concerned only with the staffing of the project, and so on). Any departmental communication within the project will be carried out by the departmental managers.

Functional structure works mostly in small firms having a few products and/or operating in a few markets. Such a structure promotes efficiency and quality because it creates specialists or professionals within each functional unit. As the firms begin to grow and the strategy becomes more complex, the functional structure can be less efficient and even problematic. The narrow specialization that is demanded by this structure can make individuals become too focused; potentially they can lose sight of customers' needs and other demands that are important for success.

The Projectized Organization

The polar opposite of the functional structure, the projectized structure, will see teams that focus primarily on projects. See Figure 3.2.

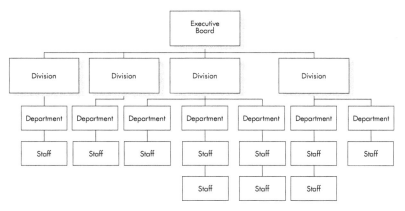

Figure 3.1 Functional structure. From: Project Management Institute, A Guide to the Project Management Body of Knowledge (PMBOK® Guide)—Third Edition, *Project Management Institute, Inc., 2004. Copyright and all rights reserved. Material from this publication has been reproduced with the permission of PMI.*

When firms arc involved in multiple markets or have a large number of product lines that require cross-functional interaction, such a framework is appropriate for handling demands. In this structure, each project is run as a separate, autonomous unit, and decision making becomes timely and effective. The project manager, having total control of the allocated resources and budget, runs the group as a profit-and-loss center.

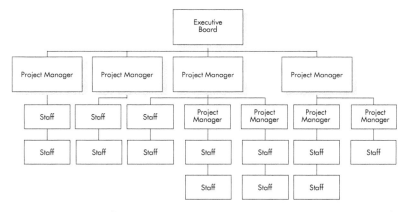

Figure 3.2 Projectized structure. From: Project Management Institute, A Guide to the Project Management Body of Knowledge (PMBOK® Guide)—Third Edition, *Project Management Institute, Inc., 2004. Copyright and all rights reserved. Material from this publication has been reproduced with the permission of PMI.*

Although there are significant advantages for having a projectized structure, the framework is not without fault. At the end of the day, there is a limit to the amount of resources available to the whole company, and, because resources are often allocated based on relative performance, the shortfall can generate internal competition among the divisions. Furthermore, keeping the divisions autonomous with full functional capabilities means that there will be a duplication of activities across the organization and that can be expensive.

The Matrix Organization

Matrix structure is basically a combination of functional and projectized structure. It attempts to capture the benefits of both previously discussed structures. However, just like the other two structures, a matrix structure also has its own disadvantages. In a matrix structure, two reporting channels exist in parallel. For example, a certain Project A might need an accountant, who will be seconded from the finance department. In such a situation, the accountant will have to report back not only to the project manager of Project A, but also to the manager of the finance department. Needless to say, this may create confusion and competition for resources.

However, these disadvantages can be justified by the benefits: faster and better responses for unpredictable and complex challenges. Considering today's business environment, such a capability is necessary for an organization to sustain its competitive advantage. Understanding that the success of a matrix structure hinges on the firm's ability to share, constant negotiation and communication between managers are important. If implemented correctly, the matrix structure can foster a strong, more tight-knit organization.

The matrix structure is broken down into three types: weak matrix structure, balanced matrix structure, and strong matrix structure. Each has a varying degree of project orientation vis-à-vis functional orientation.

◘ Generally, a *weak matrix structure* (see Figure 3.3) sees staff from across the organization work on different projects but still report within the departmental hierarchy. No one is specifically assigned to be the project manager, and the person who gets to coordinate the tasks will have minimum control of resources and will not be responsible for the project budget. Individual staff within the project will report to their respective functional managers.

◘ A *balanced matrix structure* sees a project as having a project manager with more authority over resources and limited control over the budget (see Figure 3.4). However, the reporting hierarchy generally still moves along the functional lines. In other words, project managers are still working under a functional division and are reporting to the manager of that division.

◘ In a *strong matrix structure* format, the project manager is able to exercise considerable control over resources and budget (i.e., projects are managed by the project managers).

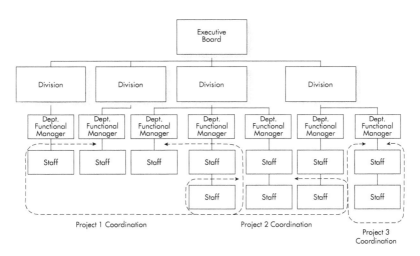

Figure 3.3 Weak matrix structure. From: Project Management Institute, A Guide to the Project Management Body of Knowledge (PMBOK® Guide)—Third Edition, *Project Management Institute, Inc., 2004. Copyright and all rights reserved. Material from this publication has been reproduced with the permission of PMI.*

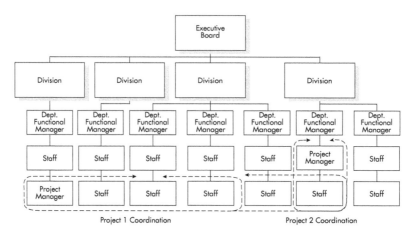

Figure 3.4 Balanced matrix structure. From: Project Management Institute, A Guide to the Project Management Body of Knowledge (PMBOK® Guide)—Third Edition, *Project Management Institute, Inc., 2004. Copyright and all rights reserved. Material from this publication has been reproduced with the permission of PMI.*

In this structure, both the project manager and the project staff may be sourced either from inside or outside the company (outsourced or temporary external staff). Such an arrangement allows for a clever use of scarce resources because, once the project is over, internal staff can return to their original divisions and temporary external project staff can either be reassigned or deployed. This type of approach to project management has become more popular because it enables resources and subject matter experts (SMEs) to be shared across departments, thereby reducing the need to build multidisciplinary teams in all areas of the organization. See Figure 3.5.

In this structure, the project personnel will not be reporting to any functional managers. Instead, they will report directly to the executive board. This is where the presence of a PMO will come in handy (as discussed later) because the PMO can handle the management of projects more efficiently than if it is handled by the executive boards, which have their own responsibilities.

Table 3.1 summarizes how the various organizational structures set the ground rule for the PMO's role. It shows how the different

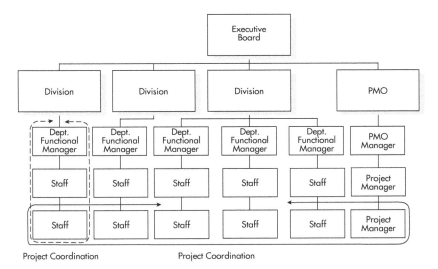

Project Coordination   Project Coordination

Figure 3.5 Strong matrix structure. From: Project Management Institute, A Guide to the Project Management Body of Knowledge (PMBOK® Guide)—Third Edition, *Project Management Institute, Inc., 2004. Copyright and all rights reserved. Material from this publication has been reproduced with the permission of PMI.*

structures allow for different levels of authority for the PMO. From this table, we can see that organizations that already adopt a balanced matrix, strong matrix, and projectized structure are generally more open to incorporating the PMO as a part of them. Organizations that do not yet have strong project activities (i.e., those with

Table 3.1 Effects of Organizational Structures on the PMO

Effect	Functional Structure	Weak Matrix	Balanced Matrix	Strong Matrix	Projectized Structure
PMO's level of authority	None	Limited	Limited to moderate	Moderate to high	High
PMO's control over resources	None	Limited	Limited to moderate	Moderate to high	High
PMO's control over budget	None	None	Limited	Moderate to high	High
PMO's role in the company	Advisory	Advisory	Advisory to limited	Moderate to high	High

Source: Adapted from Project Management Institute, *A Guide to the Project Management Body of Knowledge (PMBOK® Guide)—Third Edition,* Project Management Institute, Inc., 2004. Copyright and all rights reserved. Material from this publication has been reproduced with the permission of PMI.

Making a Case for PMO: PMO and the Organization's Structure

Organizational structure describes the way responsibilities, tasks, and people are organized (Daft, 2003), that is, the authority, relationship, and hierarchy among all the components of the organization. However, changes or restructuring, such as the incorporation of PMO into the organization, may occur from time to time due to external and internal factors. Prior to changing the organization's structure, the company's decision makers have to ask several questions (adapted from Carpenter and Sanders, 2009):

- Is the organization's current structure appropriate for the new strategy that incorporates a PMO?
- Can the current reporting relationship and delegation of authority support the incorporation of a PMO?
- Is the organization structure too centralized or decentralized for a PMO to be successfully implemented?

If the current structure is not conducive for the PMO, then the executive board needs to decide what it will do to improve it.

Going back to FAS Inc., the introduction of the Program Management Office forced the executive team to consider the company structure. Paul Witten noticed that the organization was totally functional in nature, with each product owned and operated by a specific department (or silo). Any projects requiring cross-organizational cooperation had to be communicated via the silo manager. The organization had grown to a size where it was necessary for departments to share resources and knowledge, but the current structure did not allow for that. This prompted a review of each department's functional responsibilities by the PMO. One thing that became apparent during the evaluation was that the teams were very loyal to their respective units. The PMO worked with the management team to determine which structure would best suit the company. They determined at the outset that the company had outgrown the functional management model. They also ruled out a totally projectized format because there was a strong loyalty to the old functional structures (especially concerning people's need to belong to a unit).

After some review, Paul, working with the department managers, decided to introduce a strong matrix approach to FAS Inc.'s project management. The plan was to have the teams still report to their various departments and managers, but they would also report on a project level to the assigned project manager, who would be responsible for the budget and resource allocation. The teams would be made up of people from throughout the organization and would exist for the duration of the project. The benefits were twofold: First, resources could be efficiently shared across projects, increasing the amount of work that could be completed. Second, ownership and accountability were easier to implement and track. (No longer did responsibility get hidden in a silo!)

---

functional structure and weak matrix) rarely need a PMO, but they may need a certain level of project coordination functions similar to those carried out by the PMO (more on changes and the organizations' culture in Chapter 17).

PMO Capability Level

After reviewing these different characteristics of various structures, readers should have a feel by now which type of structure your organization adopts. Before you begin to determine the best position to locate the PMO in the hierarchy, you should consider a number of factors, such as the organization's culture, size, and financial capacity, because they all determine the PMO's capability level (i.e., what the PMO's authority and roles will be). The following is the different levels commonly used to indicate a PMO's capability:

- *Level 1:* The PMO acts as a liaison between the Project Offices and the executive board for administrative purposes only (e.g., providing a summary report of the progress of all projects in the organization to the executive board, assisting with project issues escalation, and so on). In other words, Level 1 PMO adopts a reactive approach instead of the proactive approach of a Level 2 or Level 3 PMO.

- *Level 2:* The PMO goes beyond providing support and has the authority to implement actions that improve the organization's project management capacity and capability (e.g., standardizing the organization's project management process, providing project management training, and so on).

- *Level 3:* The PMO does not act only as an independent body with authority to lead the project environment, but also as a center of excellence. Thus, it directly contributes to the organization's discussions on strategy, and it takes actions to implement those strategies through projects to create competitive advantages for the organization.

Level 3 involvement of the PMO is what organizations should aspire to. At this level, the PMO can generate substantial benefits that would not only assist the organization in launching its current strategies but also help build a platform for future strategies to be developed and implemented. Over time, a company can gradually move from Level 1 to Level 3 as it becomes more comfortable with the notion and experience the benefits.

Level 1 PMO

Level 1 involvement is mostly a support role, and the PMO can operate more effectively as a unit under, for example, the finance department. From a cost standpoint this arrangement is very efficient and the direct reporting of the PMO manager to the department head facilitates decision making. The administrative support provided by the PMO can be standardized to a large extent, possibly generating further efficiency for the unit. Under these circumstances, the PMO will most likely be categorized as a cost center with a certain budget to maintain its operation. See Figure 3.6.

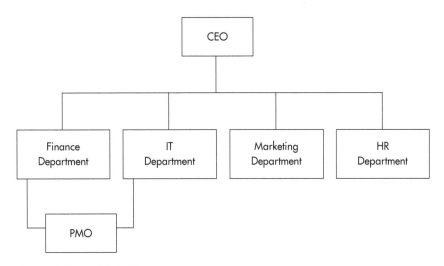

Figure 3.6 Level 1 PMO.

Level 2 PMO

When the organization has more capacity and needs a more mature PMO, then having the PMO as a separate independent department—with the PMO Manager reporting directly to the CEO—might be desirable.

The PMO's status is elevated to those of the other departments'. In doing so, the organization sends the message that the PMO is as equally important as the other departments. It is now directly responsible for the performance of the organization as a whole. In this scenario, the PMO is a key component of the value chain of the organization. Having access to the CEO or to the top management team also offers the PMO some leeway to make quick decisions related to the planning, implementation, and coordination of projects. See Figure 3.7.

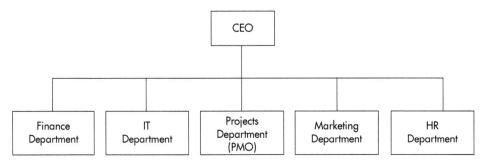

Figure 3.7 Level 2 PMO: Functional.

Some Level 2 PMOs occur in a matrix structure (see Figure 3.8), in which the PMO operates under two different departments (e.g., finance and IT). In this example, the PMO's manager reports to the manager of the finance department and the manager of the IT department, and the cost of running the PMO is borne by both departments.

As already explained, this arrangement more often than not results in confusion and office politics. The PMO simultaneously reporting to two different departments can work only when the departments have a strong level of horizontal coordination and the mind-set for sharing the PMO's work. If the departments engage in destructive behavior, trying to establish supremacy over the other, then the PMO's work (and the rest of the organization) will suffer. However, as we have explained, although a dual reporting relationship undoubtedly increases complexity and costs, if implemented properly, it can generate numerous benefits to the company.

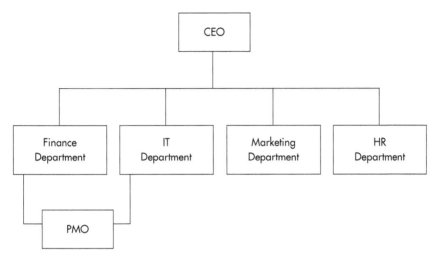

Figure 3.8 Level 2 PMO: Matrix.

Level 3 PMO

A Level 3 PMO acts as a separate department, just like Level 2 PMOs. The only difference is that the PMO acts with an expanded capacity as the center of excellence. As such, the PMO is responsible for providing strategic oversight; it often becomes the catalyst for new business strategy, while acting as the focal point for supporting the organization's projects and continuously improving the organization's capability in project delivery. In this capacity, the PMO's web of interaction becomes wider. It interacts upward with the CEO and management, horizontally with other department heads, inwardly with project participants within the organization, and outwardly with other centers of excellence and other external bodies. See Figure 3.9.

The introduction of any changes (such as the creation of a PMO) will be met with resistance at many levels. Thus, it is essential that when creating a Program Management Office, a plan (discussed in Chapter 17) is put into place to recognize and address the challenges as soon as possible. Because opposition to change is primarily emotional, it is key that any plan should be honest and forthright about

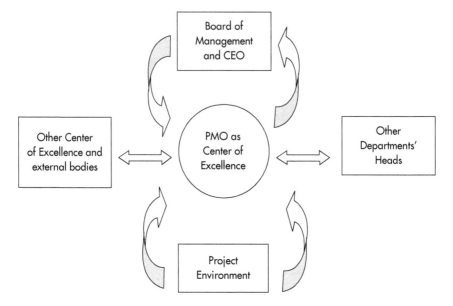

Figure 3.9 Level 3 PMO: Interaction as the center of excellence.

how the transformation will affect those involved both professionally and personally. PMO initiators must ensure that all concerns are addressed in a context that will connect the upheaval to the perceived benefits at an individual and corporate level.

Inevitably, when an organizational change is implemented, staffing arrangements and responsibilities will be adjusted. As a result, it is recommended that the approach be staged; the introduction of all changes at once, like a big bang, may not have a successful outcome. A staged introduction and cooperative movement between the PMO and functional teams, with both working alongside in harmony, is a more reasonable approach at the outset.

Key to the successful introduction of the Project Management Office will be advocacy by senior management. If they are seen to support the Office and make a point to communicate their endorsement to the teams who will work with it, eventually many barriers to acceptance will be removed. It is important for the executive team to both utilize and evangelize the PMO. By continually linking the benefits of the PMO to the goals and objectives of the individual (e.g., career enhancement) and of the organization as a whole (e.g., improvement in the organization's bottom line), a personal connection can be made and changes can be carried out more smoothly.

Conclusion

In this chapter, we have introduced the readers to the ample benefits that a PMO can provide to your organizations. We then provided guidance on how to ensure that the decision to establish a PMO in one's organization is a wise business decision. We also looked at the various structures commonly adopted by organizations, so that readers can identify which category their organizations fall into and thus gauge for themselves the PMO's capability level that will suit their organizations the most.

Assuming that readers now have firm ideas on what type of PMO is needed, the following chapters will provide valuable information on the various roles and activities commonly carried out by a PMO.

5 Things You Need to Remember from This Chapter

1. The various questions on the organization's structure, culture, capacity, and capability that decision makers need to answer before incorporating a PMO into their organization

2. The various organizational structures commonly adopted by organizations, and identifying which one is adopted by your company

3. The different levels of PMO capability

4. The factors to consider in deciding on the PMO level that is most suited for your organization

5. The type of challenges and resistance the PMO will face when it is first implemented and how to overcome them

PART II
THE CENTRAL ORGANIZER

Customer Management

The bottom line of a PMO's existence is to improve the standard of services provided by project managers to the rest of the organization (i.e., the customers). Consequently, the PMO must obviously include customer relationship management (CRM) in its operation. In this chapter, we will look at who the PMO's customers are, the best customer management approach for the PMO, the PMO's tasks in carrying out its CRM role, and the measure for the PMO's performance in managing its customers.

The PMO's Customers

We need to first define who the customers are. *Collins Gem Thesaurus* defines the word "customer" as "buyer, client, consumer, purchaser." In the program management office context, a PMO has both internal customers (the project teams themselves) and external customers (the rest of the organization).

Because the project teams are the ones who deal directly with the external customers (in a way, they are the PMO's conduit to the rest of the organization), the PMO must first ensure that it serves its internal customers well before it can serve the rest of the organization to the best of its capability.

Customer-Centric Approach for the PMO

The PMO's responsibility is multifaceted when it comes to customer service. The PMO is an internal champion for the customers, making sure that their views are heard and taken into account. Yet, the PMO is also in a position to offer and sell solutions to the customers (e.g., new ways to cut project costs, project tools and processes to assist the customers in achieving better quality products, and so on). Because of this commitment, they have to form a partnership with the customers, sharing information and capabilities. The following section discusses the various facets of the so-called customer-centric approach that the PMO manager should consider.

In today's business environment, the customer has an increased expectation to interact in real time or near real time. This need for instant interaction applies very well to the project teams. They want answers to their questions quickly and accurately. The PMO may not always react in real time but should be prepared to respond promptly. Thus, the PMO manager has to be committed to understanding the customers and anticipating their needs by keeping abreast of any changes in the industry that may affect the organization.

The essence of the customer-centric approach is customer engagement. In planning and executing a project, the PMO manager's task is first to understand what the customer needs and then to develop the most suitable approach for the project. For example, a software development project might require a project manager with specific programming experience. In the customer-centric approach, the PMO manager will go beyond this specific criterion by considering other aspects, such as personality fit, before assigning a manager to the project. Adopting a customer-centric approach will likely deliver the most consistent and positive customer experiences.

Taking a customer-oriented approach as opposed to a strict project or product orientation may require a paradigm shift. Taking such an approach does not mean neglecting the focus on the final product for the sake of fulfilling customers' requests (which, likely or not, can change so often that it will exhaust the PMO's time and resources). Rather, it means that, in making decisions, the PMO should include the customer's views and needs as valuable inputs.

In some circumstances, the PMO will be asked to put priority on some projects. Since such a situation can create conflicts between the different departments, the PMO manager should seek out the commitment and buy-in from the executive board. Not only that, putting a high priority on different customers will require greater access by the PMO to the organization's resources, structures, and processes.

The need for a PMO sponsor from the executive board is highlighted in the "customer-centric approach" since cross-functional and cross-departmental cooperation is critical to successful interaction with the customers. For example, it is inevitable that not everything works according to plan in a project setting. A sponsor who understands that and who also realizes the benefits of customer relations will help smooth over much of the resistance and organizational barriers for the PMO. The sponsor should be willing to take risks alongside the PMO to handle challenges.

Another key reason a sponsor is vital to the PMO's customer management is that a sponsor has the ability to keep the customer relations approach visible at all levels of the company. The sponsor should be positive and help keep all the stakeholders' expectations as realistic as possible. The PMO, on the other hand, should keep the sponsor informed on what is going on. Keeping the sponsor informed doesn't mean burdening the person with all kinds of problems to solve. Rather, the PMO managers should use the sponsor as infrequently as possible, primarily to deal with the most difficult problems and bottlenecks. The more the PMO can accomplish on its own, the more confidence the sponsor will have in the PMO's ability in managing its customers.

In customer management, the PMO has to look at the wider picture in devising ways to serve the rest of the organization. Different managers, departments, and business units have a stake in the success of each project. It is the PMO's role to identify and meet their needs as part of the CRM agenda.

The PMO's customer-centric approach can be summed up in three basic steps:

◘ *Customer Identification.* To better serve its customers, the PMO needs to understand them. The PMO should answer such questions as:

Who are the customers?

Which departments are they from?

What do they need?

Customer information is an asset that should be inventoried and managed. It is an important component for building loyalty. Without the necessary information, it is impossible to build strong relationships.

◘ *Customer Management.* Any project activities (new product development, process improvement, service delivery, and so on) will almost definitely include some degree of customers' participation, which warrants the PMO's involvement. The PMO manager has to balance the involvements of the customers and the managers so that both parties feel that their voices are heard and that they are partners attempting to achieve success. With the aim of ensuring customers' satisfaction, the PMO's tasks vary from facilitating project dispute resolution (prior to escalating the issue) to managing customer interaction on intraprojects. The dispute-resolution process can be time-consuming and can test the patience of all parties involved. The PMO as a facilitator has to manage the process so that everyone's focus remains on the projects while an amicable resolution takes shape.

◻ *Customer Evaluation.* The aim of the whole CRM practice is customer satisfaction, which has to be measured for the PMO to know how successful is its approach. At the PMO's discretion (in consultation with project managers), customer evaluations can be carried out in the interim or at project completion. Evaluation should be done formally (through either a customer feedback report, a survey, or a meeting) with the results recorded and analyzed for service improvements. The purpose of the feedback or survey is to understand what is working for the customer and what isn't.

The PMO's CRM Activities

What specifically does CRM mean for the PMO? The following tasks outline the PMO's day-to-day activities in its customer management role:

◻ *To build long-term value for the firm by increasing the value of the customers.* The customers add value to the organization through the projects they sponsor and implement, and each project is to add value to the company's bottom line.

◻ *To gather information, to understand and meet the needs of the customers more effectively.* Information is the key ingredient for the CRM approach to take hold. Various customer-related data (customer identification, profile, transaction, and queries) will be collected. Through information generation and sharing, the PMO can understand its customers better, thus making its services more efficient and reducing the cost of servicing the clients.

◻ *To use software tools to allow communication and information to flow.* These are essentially technologies that enable the CRM to work in the PMO. Examples are automation tools, website development, and analytical and management tools. Also, the PMO can evaluate the appropriateness of networking and integrating applications and databases.

- *To develop the processes for delivering efficient and appropriate experiences to the customers.* The PMO needs to identify and eliminate any process disconnects that may hamper the interaction with customers. For example, are there any obstacles in the communication flow between the PMO and the customer? What communications means (e.g., telephone, e-mail, and so on) can be adopted? The interaction processes should be integrated and rationalized from the customer's point of view as much as possible.

- *To train the PMO staff so that they can deliver top-notch experiences for the customers.* Ultimately, the people power the whole system. Therefore, training and education have to be arranged, new cutting-edge tools must be supplied, and measurements and rewards must be provided for success.

- *To establish CRM guidelines for all project teams to follow.* These may include, for example, an organization-wide template that can be used to capture customers' requirements, a standard customer contract form (outlining both the PMO's and the customers' roles and responsibilities), and guidelines on handling customers' feedback.

- *To answer customer relations queries coming from the project team.* The questions could be related to the specific projects, the people, and the processes. These concerns have to be addressed as promptly and efficiently as possible.

- *To apply more resources to customers needing more help from the PMO.* Of course, resource availability, cost, and funding must still be taken into account.

Although some of these activities may be frequent and somewhat routine, they are no less important. The proper handling of customer transactions can have a lasting impact on how well the projects perform. The PMO and the project managers will have to carefully manage both the day-to-day routine as well as the nonroutine strategic activities.

Performance Measure for
Customer Relationship

To measure the effectiveness of the customer initiatives and to create accountability for customers, the PMO should consider some baseline performance. The manager must ask which key performance indicators (KPIs) will be measured to know the results of the initiatives. The Project Offices, in consultation with the PMO, can develop specific measures highlighting customers' needs and implement those within the project environment. The measures should help evaluate the results of the project as compared to its stated goals.

Aim for Excellent
Customer Management

It is the responsibility of the PMO staff to understand what their customers expect from them. The main goal must be satisfying their needs. The following are a couple of points to remember to achieve excellent customer management:

- *Always treat customers with the respect they deserve.*
  Portraying a sense of superiority or showing disdain to customers can only lead to distrust and conflict. Customers are very much part of the project, and it is through their interaction that the PMO can ensure success. Every time a contact is made with the customers, it should be viewed as an opportunity to learn more about them and the tasks they do.

Making a Case for PMO: PMO and Client Services

Greenberg (2004) recommends three different metrics for customers: customer-specific metrics, diagnostic metrics, and outcome metrics.

◘ *Customer-specific metrics* focus on client's needs and issues that drive their motivation to do business with a company.

◘ *Diagnostic metrics* deal with the nature of the customer's experience when doing business with a company.

◘ *Outcome metrics* emphasize the net outcome of the relationship between the customer and the firm.

Back in FAS Inc. offices, the sales teams regularly visited existing clients to discuss upcoming enhancements to the product suite. Director of Sales James Holland tried, whenever possible, to attend the calls when a deal would be closing. He noticed often that his team knew the product very well but were unsure of the technical aspects of the updates. Sometimes this created problems at software implementation time when the new processes were rolled out to the customer. Often questions came up regarding data mapping and functionality that had been previously covered in meetings. In one case, data-cleansing services had been promised but were not part of the offered package, resulting in an argument over scope and cost between the sales department and the systems team that was escalated all the way to CEO David Strassen.

David asked Bill Clements, a senior project manager, to do the work without charge. He also convened a meeting with the PMO for systems and sales to see whether anything could be done to make sure that this did not happen in the future. When they got together they identified several problems. Understandably, the strength of the sales team was not technical. Also, they needed some help in the explanation of the data intricacies that were a component of the software.

The discussions led Paul Witten, the PMO manager, to realize that the issue was not with the organization's client, but with the relationship between the two of the internal customers of the PMO itself: sales and systems. The old departmental model, which had been used in the past, was proving hard to break free from. To solve this problem, Paul asked Bill to allow a systems expert to attend sales meetings when there may be technical questions (with the understanding that they wear a tie). He also told the sales team to ensure that they attend project meetings that were about updates to products when they were considered a stakeholder. The PMO committed to making sure what was agreed to be processed and monitored.

- *Every time there is a call or a complaint from the customer, the PMO manager must make an all-out effort to listen to exactly what the problem is.* The manager should not presume to know what the problem is based on a call. The customer should be allowed to explain or demonstrate what caused the call to the PMO. Being patient and listening carefully to customers sends a signal that the manager has the honest intention to solve the problem. Customers will feel more comfortable and may even offer ideas to assist in the solution.

- *All suggestions from the customers to improve the service and the project should be taken seriously.* Because the goal is to make sure that the project management process is easier and that customers require less support, the PMO manager must make an effort to listen to the suggestions and record them for future consideration.

◘ *There must be follow-up on problem resolution.* When confronted with a request to assist a customer, the PMO must pursue the issue until the customer is fully satisfied. The PMO should follow up with the customers to see how well the problem was handled. This is a way to improve service and to demonstrate how serious the Office is about rectifying the problems. After all, these actions will lead directly to customer satisfaction and how the PMO is perceived by the customers in the long run.

◘ *Open, frequent, and honest communications can ensure support for the PMO.* Communication, as in so many other areas of business, is crucial. Internal communications, using various tools like e-mail, intranet, bulletin boards, and meetings, are a must. The PMO manager must explain properly what measures have been taken for the issues brought forth by customers. Furthermore, educating the customers means reducing the likelihood of a similar issue occurring in the future.

Conclusion

Building customer loyalty can take a lot of investment, in both time and money, but the payoff can be enormous for the organization. High customer loyalty will help ensure long-term strategic competitiveness through continuous project improvements.

5 Things You Need to Remember from This Chapter

1. The importance of identifying the PMO's customers

2. The PMO's role and responsibility in managing customer relations

3. What it means for the PMO to adopt a customer-oriented approach

4. The three key performance indicators (KPIs) to measure the level of customer satisfaction

5. The various actions the PMO can take to ensure excellent customer service

Vendor Management

More often than not, every project requires the service of one or more vendors or contractors. They are brought into the project for the following reasons:

- They bring in specialized knowledge and skills not available in the organization.

- They fill temporarily vacant positions.

- They provide extra human resources that can be deployed once the project is over.

- They may act as independent advisors to the project executives.

Considering the fact that an organization may have multiple projects running at the same time, each employing its own vendors or contractors, vendor management becomes an important task for the PMO to fulfill. This chapter looks at selecting vendors, developing relationships with vendors, and other tasks involved in the PMO's vendor management role in detail.

The PMO's Relationship with Vendors

The relationship between the PMO and the vendors requires a series of interactions. For small projects, the vendors may have initial discussions with the PMO about a project, which subsequently lead to the award of the contract. For large contracts, the process is usually complex, and normally the bidding process is competitive.

In contract discussions, a number of issues must be negotiated and agreed to: project budget and funding for vendors go hand in hand, project time frame must be set to allow the vendor to complete his or her job with reasonable effort, and, on top of that, vendor availability can become an issue when a suitable vendor has been selected but cannot join in the project immediately. All of these issues indicate yet another area where a PMO can add value to the organization. With this in mind, it is obvious that the PMO's main goal in vendor management is to optimize the value of the vendors and contractors for the projects, which the PMO can achieve through the implementation of standardized selection, monitoring, and review processes (discussed later in this chapter).

The PMO's Vendor Management Tasks

From the preceding discussion, it is obvious that the PMO's relationship with the vendor can be complicated. The following section looks at a number of tasks the PMO needs to carry out to ensure good working relationships with vendors.

Identify the Need for Qualified Vendors and Investigate Market Availability

The PMO, in collaboration with project managers, determines the nature of vendors and contractors needed to support the success of the projects within the organization. This discussion should include consideration of who and what is needed, the frequency of engagement, and contract duration. The PMO should have a clear understanding of the goals and requirements. If there is any confusion about what is expected, the final outcome of the work will likely be disappointing. Also, it may be very difficult later to manage the contract with the vendors if too many changes are being made.

The PMO will probably have to develop a business case for contracting the vendors. Such a business case should address questions like the following:

- What are the assumptions being made about the project activities?

- What are the costs and benefits for employing the vendors?

- Is the purpose primarily to save costs, transfer risks, or avoid capital expenditure?

- Could the company be trying to solve a complex strategic problem (e.g., difficulty in obtaining enough employees in an area of scarce skills, gaining better access to the technology in a fast-developing field, tying in to new sources of innovation, and so on), which may require a long-term solution (in which case contracting a vendor might be a Band-Aid® solution that will not last)?

Without clear answers to these questions, it is difficult, if not impossible, to evaluate the decision to contract, or to ensure that the right vendors are selected.

Once the PMO is aware of the needs for vendors, the next step is to focus its search on suitable suppliers in the market. This exercise forces the PMO to be aware of the latest practices and developments in the project management field. PMO managers have to continuously update their knowledge of the state of the art in the field as it relates to different vendors. Based on the relevant information, the PMO will select the vendors and contractors equipped with corresponding skills. Important questions that should be asked at this stage are:

◘ What differentiation can the vendor offer to the project?

◘ Can the vendor offer a unique package or an innovative solution that will add value to the project?

◘ Is the vendor a good fit with the organization (in terms of work ethic, strategy, and so on)?

Thinking about these early on will help choose the most appropriate vendor for the work.

Maintain Vendor Information

Once the need for a vendor is identified, and the project and PMO managers have an idea of the type of vendors they would like to bring on board, they will need a list of suitable candidates. The management of vendor information is a vital function in optimizing vendors' and contractors' usefulness. The efficient management of this practice can be achieved only when the PMO centralizes the information database within the project management environment. Developing the database needs intelligence gathering done by desk research, informal discussion, and inquiries.

The database should have the following characteristics:

1. *It should include all information related to all vendors and contractors, either in the past or currently engaged.* Such data may include the vendors' and contractors' names, which projects they worked or are working on, the length of their contracts, a list of their specific skills and abilities, their fee rates, and their project performance. It is critical that the database provides sufficient information to help the managers understand each vendor's competence and track record. The availability of the information will also assist project managers in searching out suitable vendors for upcoming projects (i.e., it is a long-term investment). In addition, the database will help clarify any existing gaps between needs and resources, and

this information can be useful input for the strategic resource planning of the PMO and the company.

2. *Along the same lines, the PMO can take a proactive approach to expand the available list.* Based on a general awareness of project needs, the PMO can compile data regarding potential suitable vendors available in the market. The PMO can then prequalify them through a screening process, thus making them available for selection by project managers. Prequalification can save a lot of money and work by eliminating vendors who clearly cannot match the needs of the assignments in terms of capacity, experience, financial resources, and competence. This exercise anticipates the need for specific skills not encountered.

Develop Vendor Management Guidelines

The engagement of different vendors and contractors by different project offices within an organization warrants the need for common guidelines. These guidelines will set the expectations and standards, which will be used for managing the vendors and contractors during work. The availability of such a standard facilitates an effective handling of vendors and contractors, because it precludes project managers from reinventing the wheel for every new project.

Considering the different nature of various projects within the organization, the guidelines need to be developed with project managers so that they meet the managers' needs. The PMO is also responsible for promoting familiarity with the overall guidelines to the project managers and vendors or contractors because this may be important for its successful implementation.

In general, vendor management guidelines should include the following elements:

- *How to develop cost estimates for vendor and contractor engagements.* Such estimates are a necessary reference before going through a bidding process or even obtaining quotes from various service providers. The exercise requires project managers to have a general knowledge of the vendors' and contractors' rates and some experience in estimating how long it will take a vendor or contractor to complete the project.

◻ *Procedures on vendor and contractor selection, which are summarized in the following:*

- Identification of the necessary qualifications (skills, academic, experience) to add value to the project

- Way to solicit proposals, whether in an open bid (advertised in a public newspaper), closed bid (invitations issued to a select few), or direct request (to one service provider only). For large long-term projects that may last several years, it may be wise to invite only a few vendors who fulfill stringent criteria to make a formal bid, in order to simplify the process. The bid process should also provide the opportunity for the PMO to explore the issues together with potential vendors. In addition, it offers a chance to see whether there is a problem of compatible personalities and work cultures.

- Procedure for evaluating proposals. Instead of looking solely at the figures, weights should be assigned to such factors as experience in completing similar projects, experience working with the organization, and whether the price quoted falls within the acceptable range.

- Procedure to award bids to successful vendors and a debriefing procedure to unsuccessful vendors

◻ *How to manage a vendor contract.* The guideline should include (but not be limited to) the following:

- Procedure for setting contract terms and conditions. This part may seem bureaucratic and wordy, but it is important to make sure that there is no room for ambiguity. Legal advice should be sought to write the procedure.

- Procedure to manage contract variation (e.g., changes to contract duration, cost, scope, and so on), where such variation may be initiated by either side.

- Deliverables management. The contract should outline whether the organization will impose a penalty if the deliverables are not completed within the agreed duration and with the required level of quality.

- Invoice payment procedure. For organizations with strong project structure, this should be handled by each project office in collaboration with the accounting department.

- Procedure for dispute resolution. Generally speaking, the parties should enter into a contract in the expectation that issues, disputes, difficulties, and unexpected developments will be resolved fairly so as not to bring undue advantage or disadvantage to either side. Fairness should reflect a reasonable and balanced view of the parties' obligations and commitment to each other, as listed in the contract.

- Communication guidelines between the vendors or contractors and the client (whether it will include regular meetings, reports, and the like). There should be multiple levels of contact. At the top, the project manager must be accessible and hold regular formal (meetings) and informal contacts. Also, the PMO and the respective project managers should hold periodic formal meetings, at which appropriate-level managers from the vendors can participate to discuss progress, deal with issues, and anticipate problems. At a lower level, there has to be accessible communication links between the vendor and project staffs to ensure that immediate problems are resolved and progress is maintained.

◻ *Postcontract activities with an emphasis on reviewing the vendor's or contractor's performance and handling of procedures.* The vendors know they will be held to the quality, performance, and service levels agreed to at the outset. Typically, the requirements for quality increase as the project's vulnerability increases, such as in a situation where poor quality work by the vendor may lead to disastrous consequences for the company. Given this scenario, the PMO and the project offices must put a lot of emphasis on documenting the vendors' work for quality management purposes. Keep in mind that this is a form of tacit knowledge that, if properly recorded and disseminated, can help the projects and the company to build advantages (refer to Chapter 8). In addition, the project managers must decide on the type of reviews and discussion, as a way of monitoring performance. Control and evaluation are important for securing a meaningful association with the vendors.

Conclusion

Relationships with vendors go deeper than contract fulfillment. When the project requires vendors and employees to work as partners, it is important to look for compatibility. The PMO and the individual projects must develop a partnership mentality and seek the same from the vendor. Otherwise, the chance for success will be compromised. Work ethics or personality clashes can lead to project delays, budget overshoot, and client dissatisfaction. A good working relationship based on trust eliminates trivial disputes and opens the door to business opportunities. From time to time, both sides can participate in discussions on how to improve project management. New ideas and experiments can be drawn and tested. For these reasons, the PMO must take vendor management into account in its effort to add value to the organization.

Making a Case for PMO: PMO and Managing Contracts with Vendors

Paul Witten, the PMO manager, once again found himself in the middle of a dispute between a vendor and a project manager. The vendor, Dustin Kallan, had been writing product manuals as a contractor for FAS Inc. over the preceding three years. He had moved around within a number of FAS departments. He got to do that because he did good work and everyone wanted him. The project manager, Rumana Thirunavukarasu, had been working in the IT department for the last five years.

Dustin accused Rumana of breaching the vendor agreement on the scope of work. Rumana, however, believed that she had been following protocols and hadn't done anything wrong. Paul decided to read the contract for himself, and found that the wording in the contract was very vague and could be interpreted in multiple ways. He also found that every department in FAS used different templates for writing their vendor contracts. Dustin, who had worked for various departments in FAS Inc. and Rumana, who had always stayed with the IT department, obviously came to different conclusions on what the wording in the contract meant.

Paul knew that this was not an isolated incident. Disputes between project managers and vendors had been becoming more and more common. He realized that if FAS wanted to keep their good contractors, they needed to revamp their contracts. Once he helped Dustin and Rumana reach an agreement, he went off to the legal department to start the process of drafting a standard contract to be used throughout the organization.

5 Things You Need to Remember from This Chapter

1. The role of vendors in a project

2. The major activities for the PMO in managing vendors (i.e., identifying the needs for vendors, maintaining a database of vendors, selecting vendors, deploying vendors, and developing vendor management guidelines)

3. The must-include items in vendor management guidelines

4. The type of information that should be saved in the vendor database

5. The reasons having a good working relationship with vendors is so important

Communications Management

Organizational communication is a vital task for an effective PMO. To ensure project success, information and ideas need to flow flawlessly in both directions: to the managers and to the staff, inside and outside the PMO. Along with information, there is also the need for negotiation and dialogue among different parties. How might the PMO manager deal with all these communication challenges? This chapter will look at the various factors that make up good communications across various channels. Also, it will examine the PMO's roles in communications management.

The Concept of Communications Management

Success in any company relies on the information exchanges among managers, employees, customers, suppliers, and other stakeholders. Therefore, it is imperative that the leadership always maintains good communications with all parties. Since communications management is not a new field in business study, the concept has been discussed in-depth in other books. Thus, our aim in this chapter is to introduce readers to the concept of effective communications management in a successful PMO.

First, it is worthwhile to know that most corporate communication flows in four different directions: upward, downward, across, and outward (Hambrick and Cannella, 1989). In other words, PMOs will communicate upward to top managers to convey any ideas conceived in the field and downward (i.e., to the Project Offices). They will also communicate outward and across with other business units and external stakeholders (suppliers, vendors, customers, and so on).

Second, in managing proper communication flow, managers need to have a good understanding of the culture, policies, and processes of the organization. Such an understanding will provide insights about the linkages and dependencies across business units and between the firm and outside actors.

Third, the communicator must be trustworthy and credible. If people do not trust the messenger, the message may very well be lost. To develop credibility, the PMO must demonstrate a behavioral commitment through its actions, in whatever it is trying to communicate.

Finally, for communications management to be effective, the PMO must develop a clear sense of the people it serves; that is, it must be customer focused (a need that is closely related to the topic of the previous chapter) and understand what they want. Think about what the customers want to know, when they prefer to receive information, and in what form the messages should be disseminated. The PMO has to continuously monitor its customers (i.e., audience) to be able to communicate effectively and efficiently.

After a review of these principles, how can we apply them and create effective and efficient communications between the PMO and the rest of the organization? The following discussion answers that question.

Making a Case for PMO: Planning for PMO's Effective Communication

M. Young and J. E. Post, in their article "Managing to Communicate, Communicating to Manage" (1993), highlight the different factors deemed critical for communications management:

- Communicate not only what is happening, but why and how it is happening. Explain the rationale behind the decision.

- Timeliness is vital. The failure to communicate on time can lead to a loss of trust (people will feel such communication is orchestrated and not spontaneous).

- Communicate continuously. Maintain a dialogue and build trust.

FAS Inc.'s communication lines generally went one way: up. Or so CEO David Strassen feels. Sometimes he wondered whether all the people whom he worked with were paid to complain. If it wasn't the customers, it was his management team. The funny thing was that his managers felt that the flow was in the opposite direction: ideas continually coming downstream with little follow-up. When they approached Dave about issues or problems, he was too busy or too willing to leave it in their "capable hands." As Paul Witten worked to introduce the PMO, one thing he discovered was that communications stop at the department managers' doors. Rarely were team members consulted on matters that concern them. They felt that there was little feedback or support to help them, which exacerbated the problem. The support teams believed that they were the only reason that the managers had jobs (not an unusual attitude). Dave also discovered that the PMO was not seen as a help, but as an added level of bureaucracy. Once he understood the challenges Paul created a communications plan for the PMO's introduction. From this he created a template for use across the organization. His plan was simple: He would hold one stakeholder meeting per week to review project status and open issues. Here, challenges and risks could be reviewed by all attendees so that relevant actions can be taken. Second, he determined what needed to be communicated to the various stakeholder groups and put together a timetable and format for each (e-mail, issue logs, status reports, meetings, and so on). Finally, he asked David Strassen and his team to continually evangelize the introduction of the PMO and presented them with communications channels and information to support the implementation that could be used during discussions. He also asked the management team to review their functional communication strategies. He felt that improved interaction between unit leaders and team members, both up and down, would assist in the introduction of new processes within the project environment.

Communication Channels

As explained, the PMO's communication management extends in four directions. It is important for the PMO to identify in detail all of the parties involved to determine how to continuously monitor, control, and improve the communication channels between them and the PMO.

As Figure 6.1 shows, communication channels should be established between the PMO and the project-related units, as well as between the PMO and the rest of the organization. The key to success is to have open channels of communication, both vertically and horizontally. By "open channels," we suggest direct access with minimum, if at all, monitoring or filtering of information and communication. There should be no bottlenecks. Particularly between the PMO and the business units within the organization, there ought to be good horizontal communication channels (using various media such as e-mail, telephone, intranet, individual and group meetings [both formal and informal], and so on). These channels will keep the businesses abreast of the project developments that are relevant to them.

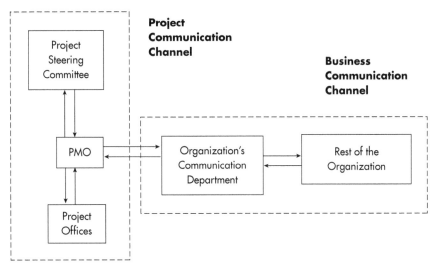

Figure 6.1 The PMO's communication channels.

The PMO, project offices, and other business units are all interdependent. The PMO has the challenge of coordinating communications with these units, and, if the coordination is not properly done, problems can result. If, for example, the internal communication between a project office and other departments is not coordinated properly, customer dissatisfaction will result. Another problem can occur when business units have a narrow orientation and are engaged in turf protection, leading to minimal communication. Also, communications can be ineffective when there are interunit conflicts whereby individuals simply don't want to cooperate.

These problems occur quite frequently among firms. Why? As Clampitt (2001) points out, there are several reasons. The office structure or design can create barriers to effective communication. Typically, rigid structures and procedures (with lots of guidelines) lead to restrictions in internal communication. Also, departments have different priorities, leading to communication problems when one department is dependent on another. Companies with rigid structures have rewards and punishments that are directly tied to the departments, and managers from other departments have very little influence on an individual's reward. In this scenario, interdepartmental communication will fail to generate high levels of enthusiasm. Finally, as the company grows, the number of communication linkages between departments increases. The complex coordination required to manage these linkages can be difficult.

So what can managers do, especially in the PMO's situation where it has to communicate with multiple projects and business units? The following ideas should be considered.

1. The PMO manager should attempt to rally employees around common goals and values. It could be customer service, competitors, or some other important theme.

2. The manager must assign top priority to achieving cooperation among departments. The value of working together must be clearly communicated.

3. Often, there is an inherent tension between information providers and receivers. The objective for the manager is to be sensitive to the needs and problems of the parties. Routine and nonroutine information should flow in a timely manner without redundancy and overload.

These ideas can be implemented through a number of avenues, such as companywide seminars to foster interactions among employees from different units, coauthoring articles, brainstorming sessions, interdepartmental agreements, tracking organizational processes, redesign procedures and structures, job rotation, job description modifications, and cross-functional teams.

Communications Audience

To be effective in organizational communications, the PMO needs to understand its audience, specifically defining (among other things) a number of its aspects:

- *Customer Profile (age range, gender, education background, work experience, and so on).* There may be limitations in terms of how far the PMO can customize the message. Still, having a profile can offer insights on how individuals and departments view communications and which factors they consider important.

- *Their Preferred Communication Media (e-mail, face-to-face, newsletters, and so on).* Managers have various communications media at their disposal. Understanding which ones are preferred and under what conditions (emergency or regular situation, select few or everyone, and so on) can make communications more effective.

- *Their Project-Related Interests.* Needless to say, the projects are the principal focus for the PMO when communicating to all relevant units. Looking at the specific interests of the business units and attempting to customize the message accordingly can help. This is also something that has to be tracked over time. The interests can change depending on the project's status and the stage of completion. This has to be taken into consideration in planning interdepartmental communications.

The PMO's Communication Roles

Upon understanding its audience, the PMO, in consultation with the stakeholders, will also need to define its role in communication management. Most large organizations already have a separate department in charge of communications management. Thus, to reach a wider audience beyond the project environment, the PMO should closely liaise with that department.

The following are some of the common activities that the PMO is responsible for in its communication management role:

- *Design of PMO's Communications Structures.* This is the hierarchy of information flow from person to person.

- *Outline of the PMO's Communications Principles and Standards.* These are driven by ethical norms and practical needs. For example, communications should be transparent, accurate, and timely.

- *Formulation of the PMO's Communications Goals.* Examples are assisting the projects to meet the deadlines, ensuring rich and quality information exchange, and so on.

- *Management and Monitoring of Information Flows in the Project Channel.* This is important for avoiding possible confusion and misunderstanding, as well as for controlling the various steps to meet the project deadlines.

- *Creation of Regular Communication Media for Constituents in Both Project and Business Environments.* An example is a monthly newsletter featuring new achievements derived from recently implemented project management tools.

- *In Liaison with the Communications Department, Creation of a Communications Management Strategy.* Ideally, this should include the development of communication goals for various audiences, a common set of goals for the general audience, a unifying theme that motivates employees across units, allocation of communication resources based on the analysis of the units, developing a structure for achieving the goals, and crisis management.

- *Continuous Improvement of Its Communication Capabilities.* This entails investments for the upgrading and maintenance of communication structure and processes.

Conclusion

Every individual and business unit in an organization has information and ideas to share. The PMO has the important role of creating a conducive project environment so that those ideas can be communicated and become projects that create competitive advantage for the organization.

5 Things You Need to Remember from This Chapter

1. The PMO's communication channels go in four different directions, connecting the PMO and the rest of the organization

2. The PMO's communication audience and the importance of understanding it

3. The possible problems that the PMO could encounter in managing the flow of communication among the different parties

4. The possible solutions for those problems

5. The tasks that the PMO is responsible for as a part of its role in managing effective communication within the project environment and with the rest of the organization

Project Office Management

We have seen in the previous chapters how the PMO uses its role to influence vendors, customers, and way of communications. However, at its most granular level, the PMO exists to drive good project practice. Without good project management process, the PMO will not be able to function. The Project Office, as the extension arm of the PMO, deals directly with the PMO's end users (i.e., the rest of the organization). Understanding their importance, we dedicated this chapter for a specific discussion on the Project Office.

The Project Office, sometimes referred to as project support office, is established at the commencement of every project to ensure that project management standards, as defined by the PMO, are implemented. Don't be confused by the term; in essence, the Project Office is the most fundamental unit in the project environment, crucial to the success of every project. As an extension of the PMO, it implements the project management principles while providing administrative support to project managers. The Project Office may be staffed internally (company resources assigned to the project) or externally (teams hired specifically for the venture).

The Project Office can be a physical location, staffed by a team supporting a specific endeavor, or it can be a virtual arrangement. For example, a Project Office may be established by generating a project request and assigning a project manager responsible for executing that effort. The Project Office structure is then determined by the type of undertaking it has been created to support. It is more likely that a physical office would be established as part of a construction project, whereas software development may require the creation of a virtual Project Office.

In this chapter we will review the operation of the Project Office, evaluating the processes it should use to successfully manage the project it supports. Included in Appendix B are templates and examples of the various project management techniques required for successful project execution and illustrations of their use. Once completed, readers will have a foundation on which to build good project management practice.

So how do the PMO and the Project Office work together? How does the organization benefit from this collaboration? Let us look at four major areas where good Project Office execution will bring success to the PMO. The Project Office will:

1. *Make certain that the project under its control is run according to best practice, as required by the PMO.* This will improve process execution, deliver improved results, and facilitate the adoption of best practices across the organization.

2. *Ensure that the required reporting information for the project (budget, schedule, and so on) is provided to the PMO within the specified timeframe to facilitate production of management reporting for the executive team.* The information collected at ground (Project Office) level from all projects is collated and analyzed by the PMO. This key information is then presented to the executive board to assist them in making strategic decisions for the company.

3. *Be supported by the PMO in every aspect of project management, including strategic direction and resource requirements.* The

PMO ensures that every Project Office (or project) has what it needs to operate efficiently and effectively.

4. *Maintain open lines of communication with the PMO (and vice versa).* This ensures that any issues can be addressed in a timely fashion.

The functionality of the office should be defined in a collaboration between the project managers and the PMO. However, industry practice dictates that it should include at least:

- Project Governance

- Project Planning and Milestone Delivery

- Project Administration

Project Governance

The Project Office acts as the frontline supervisor in implementing project management policies and procedures. Prior to the commencement of any project, it should create a project management office handbook that outlines how the project will be run. This may include a recognized set of standards that apply to all projects (e.g., a formal software development methodology). At the outset of the project, as part of the kickoff, all members of the team should familiarize themselves with these rules. As new resources are introduced at various stages, they too should become part of the handbook. The handbook is a living document and will change in form from time to time. The document should be updated when processes or team members change, budgets are amended, and other changes take place. The document may be included in the project plan or exist as a separate entity, referenced in the plan.

The handbook should contain the following elements:

- Amendment and log update.

- Statement of the objectives of the Project Office.

- Hierarchical structure of the project, including a list of the project team members, project sponsors, and other stakeholders.

- Responsibility matrix, which outlines the responsibilities of each project participant.

- Communication and reporting structure: what reports have to be produced, at what frequency, and who will be the recipients.

- Meeting structure and protocol: how many different meetings will be needed (e.g., team meetings, steering committee meetings, and so on), who will attend each meeting, and what the objective will be. Meetings can also be used as an avenue to escalate issues and risk resolution. Protocol will be used to establish rules for attendance, participation, minute taking, and so on.

- Documentation standards, including naming conventions and version control for the various documents to be used, as well as the creation of a centralized repository for all documents created. It is important to note that such details have proven to be vital in creating an efficient project management environment.

- Deliverables management procedure to ensure that each completed deliverable is reviewed and signed off by the appropriate authority.

- Change control procedure, ensuring that any change to the agreed-on project plan (either on project scope, schedule, budget, or anything else) goes through the appropriate channel where it is registered, reviewed, and signed off by the appropriate authority.

- Risk management procedure to ensure that all risks and issues are properly identified, recorded, and escalated through the appropriate channel for resolution.

- Financial control procedure: methods used for funding the project and the stages at which the funding will be reviewed and continued (if dependent on stage-based performance measures or stage gates, discussed in Chapter 12). These methods will be defined by and operate within the constraints of the organization's financial policy.

- Vendor and contractor management procedure: the day-to-day management of vendors and contractors, including performance management, contract management, and timesheet-invoice-payment approval.

- Appendices containing miscellaneous forms needed for the project.

Project Planning and Milestone Delivery

The document detailing project execution, the project plan contains the details of the project schedule, scope, deliverables, budget, and other features, and it ensures that those items are documented and agreed on. The project plan may also contain the Project Office's handbook.

The Project Office is responsible for providing support to the project team with regard to producing deliverables. Collaborating with the project team, it monitors the details of project performance. Such actions allow for early problem detection and facilitate appropriate corrective actions. The following tools are commonly used by the Project Office:

- *Work Breakdown Structure (WBS).* This is a hierarchical diagram that identifies specific deliverables for the project. The structure should be decomposed to its lowest level to include ownership, scope, milestone dates, signoff responsibilities, and the like. At this point, each deliverable will have an associated

In Praise of the PMO: Support for the Project Office

Jean Roberts, a Project Manager at FAS Inc., was continually frustrated by the lack of attention paid by remote attendees at her project meetings. Indeed it seemed sometimes as if her statements were totally ignored. The last straw came when a key participant, who asked her to move a meeting with little notice, appeared 40 minutes late and proceeded to eat his lunch without making any contribution.

Jean has heard that the recently introduced PMO at FAS Inc. would be putting together a project handbook that addresses the problem of "distracted" meeting participants. She called the office and complained about her challenges. The PMO shared the meeting rules with her, and she realized that the problems reside not just with the attendees, but with her approach to chairing the meetings as well. She didn't give her attendees enough time to prepare, had too many meetings, and had a habit of calling her project team together at the drop of a hat.

The rules provided were simple:

- Give people time to prepare.
- Start on time.
- Provide a rigid framework to operate in (for example, no cell phones, no laptops, and so on).
- Stay on message.
- Distribute minutes and action items immediately.
- Meet only when necessary.
- Stick to the same time for recurring meetings.

Based on the rules, Jean revamped her meeting approach and saw an immediate improvement in the response and interest levels of her attendees.

entry in the WBS dictionary (identified by a unique number or control account) that defines the work package (refer to Appendix B for an example).

◻ *Risk Register.* This allows the project team to identify risks that may be encountered throughout the project, to assess them, to take mitigating action, and to monitor the effects.

◻ *Change Control Process.* Should changes be required to the project plan or associated documents, processes have to be in place to formalize the updates. The changes will be requested in the form of change control requests, which will be reviewed by the relevant decision makers and either be approved or disapproved. Only approved changes should be implemented.

Examples of a template (adapted from the template documents in PRINCE2 by the Office of Government Commerce, United Kingdom) for a deliverables register, issues register, risk register, change control request, project finance record, and project status report are available in Appendix B.

Project Administration

The Project Office is designed to provide day-to-day administrative support to the project team. In doing so, it promotes an efficient project management practice. The following tasks are commonly adopted by the Project Office:

◻ *Producing the Project Status Report.* Normally prepared by the project team and distributed to the project executives and relevant stakeholders, this report shows the actual project completion status against planned schedules, deliverables, resources, and budget. When the project is lagging behind schedule, the delay must be flagged in the report and discussed in the meeting.

- *Managing the Information Repository.* The Project Office ensures accurate, consistent, and complete information on a project is properly retained or communicated to other stakeholders when necessary.

- *Managing the Facilities and Equipment.* Liaising with the organization's office manager, the Project Office makes sure that project team members have all the necessary equipment, maintain it, and return the materials to the office manager on project completion.

- *Stakeholders Management.* The Project Office is responsible for handling contracts administration (registration, filing, and so on), liaising with the finance department for invoice payment to vendors and contractors, client invoicing for project work completed, bookkeeping for all project revenues and expenditures, handling clients' feedback, and other administrative tasks.

Conclusion

The shape of the Project Office may vary from project to project, but its basic functions and strong relationship with the PMO must stay the same throughout the lifecycle of the undertaking. The Project Office exists to support project managers by liaising with the PMO to provide the support needed to execute a project successfully. The PMO relies on the Project Office to ensure that its standards and practices are carried out as part of a project and that timely and accurate reporting takes place. When functioning together as intended, they will complement each other and give the project manager the tools for success.

5 Things You Need to Remember from This Chapter

1. The Project Office may be physical or virtual depending on the type of project it supports.

2. It may be staffed by outside entities or by members of the functional team assigned to the project.

3. The Project Office exists to support both the project manager and the PMO.

4. The Project Office will provide guidelines and support for the project manager to successfully execute.

5. The principles applied by each Project Office within an organization should be uniform, reflecting the guidelines laid down by the PMO.

Project Knowledge Management

Globalization has created both advantages and challenges for today's organizations. With project teams spread across continents and time zones, it certainly has allowed for reduced costs, longer workdays, and changes in how we do business. However, although there is much to be gained, companies are forced to reconsider how their knowledge should be handled so that it can be distributed efficiently and securely while maintaining and updating it as required (Melik, 2007).

The difficulty in managing knowledge is not limited to geography. The fast turnaround of today's workforce means that staff are constantly taking their knowledge away with them when they leave the company. In his book, *The Handbook of Program Management*, James T. Brown notes that the teams involved with a program today will generally not be the same ones involved in the project five years from now. Couple that fact with the amount of knowledge lost within the organization itself. A survey conducted by Collaborative Strategies LLC found that 32 percent of time in the normal workweek is spent answering questions, and, of these questions, 54 percent have been answered before. Faced with this challenge, companies need some form of management process to avoid the loss of knowledge associated with such flux. In addition, the constantly changing business landscape means that there is always new information out there that the organization needs to keep up with to stay ahead in the game.

With this in mind, it is obvious that as the PMO includes knowledge management *in the project environment* as a part of its roles, it contributes to the organization's competitive advantage. Not only does the PMO circumvent the loss of project knowledge, but it also seeks to gain new information to advance the organization's project management capability.

In this chapter, readers will first be introduced to the concept of knowledge management, along with the benefits (both tangible and intangible) it offers. We then discuss the type of activities the PMO carries out as a part of its knowledge management function, as well as the tools and strategy needed to do so.

What Is Knowledge Management?

Peter Drucker first coined the term "knowledge worker" in his book *The Age of Discontinuity* to describe the rising workforce in the 1960s, whose contribution to organizations is that of intelligence as opposed to manual labor. Over time, this concept evolved into knowledge management, whose definition can be summed up as the practice of creating, identifying, accumulating, applying, sharing, and distributing information and ideas with the aim of achieving values through the organization's increased knowledge capacity. Such an increase allows the organization specific competitive advantages, such as more efficient operation, improved performance, and a conducive environment for innovation. As a result, knowledge management is considered a critical objective for almost all organizations, along with growth and efficiency.

Knowledge Management Advantages for the Organization

Data or information can be considered a resource, but it is what managers do with the data that results in positive or negative outcomes. As will be explained later in the chapter, the application of knowledge management is manifested in an interactive hub that not only stores information from past projects, but also facilitates an orderly exchange of ideas across all parts of the organization. The storage of such information allows project staff to learn from past mistakes, and it eliminates the need to start from scratch every time a new project is initiated. As a result, organizations can constantly improve the quality of their products and services faster and with less cost.

The advantages offered to an organization by adopting the practice of knowledge management are both tangible (like those just explained) and intangible. For example, the exercise of knowledge gathering requires input from all stakeholders, which can be turned into a team-building exercise that strengthens the organization's internal network. To sum up, when properly applied, the PMO's knowledge management function can elevate the traditional aspect of simple information exchange into a platform that nurtures efficiency and innovation (translating to competitive advantage for the organization).

The PMO's Knowledge Management Roles

Considering the benefits offered by knowledge management, it is only reasonable that it be incorporated into the organization's project management environment. To gain those benefits, the PMO needs to carry out three main roles:

1. *The Authority in the Organization's Management of Knowledge.* This role requires the PMO to implement standardized instruments that guide project participants in managing the flow of project information and documentation. In this role, the PMO may enforce processes and procedures to ensure that all important knowledge and insight from past and current projects are captured, for example, by making sure that project managers contribute to the knowledge repository regularly with all the lessons learned in their project.

2. *The Facilitator Within the Organization.* In this role, the PMO should encourage discussions among project participants to optimize the exchange of ideas. One way to achieve this is by providing training and information sessions to emphasize the importance of knowledge management to project participants. As more staff becomes aware of the purpose of knowledge management, more information can be stored and more ideas can be exchanged, in the end improving the organization's competitiveness.

3. *The Leader in Project Knowledge Management.* As a leader, the PMO will actively seek information on the latest development in the project management field to ensure that the organization's project management capability remains at the top of the field. To fulfill this role, the PMO may subscribe to industry magazines or attend conferences for the latest breakthrough in project management theories. The PMO will then take that knowledge and implement it within the organization.

To be able to successfully fulfill its role, the PMO needs to carry out the following tasks (discussed later in this chapter) to properly establish and implement the PMO's knowledge management function within the organization.

Establishing the PMO's Knowledge Management Function

These steps are required before the PMO can fully function in this role:

1. Design the knowledge management hub.

2. Determine the medium needed (e.g., electronic or paper).

3. Implement the knowledge management system.

Designing the Knowledge Management Hub

- The knowledge management hub will function as a library, and it should include as much information as possible on both current and past projects. When an old project that is already been completed suddenly fails, all related information must be reviewed to correct the problem. By the same token, when a completed project is proven to be successful, the project teams might want to learn from it.

- The hub must at a minimum contain pertinent information on existing projects that has been formally reviewed by stakeholders and approved (e.g., project progress status, goals, cost estimates, sponsor documents, research documents, product training manuals [if any], and so on).

- It must also include a complete documentation of project management policies, procedures, and guidelines that are still current.

- The outcomes of project review (i.e., the lessons learned from completed and open projects) must immediately be stored in the library.

- Project management references published by industry professionals (e.g., PMBOK, industry magazines, project management textbooks, and so on) are wonderful additions to the library.

Toward the end of this chapter, we will discuss how an organization can gather all of this information through a process called knowledge harvesting.

Determining the Medium Needed

Depending on the organization's capability, a modern, presumably electronic tool (such as the intranet) could be the answer for the demands posed by the PMO's knowledge management function, especially because a physical library alone imposes a lot of limitations (such as space, document life span, and so on). With such a tool, there is also the potential for selectively extending the system access to external project participants (stakeholders from outside the organization) as a way of providing high-quality and efficient knowledge transfer, which otherwise could be cumbersome.

An online, intranet-type electronic tool has been used by various companies to facilitate organizational knowledge and learning. For example, the electronic site will have an up-to-date database containing details of every project: the participants, the nature of the project, the outcome, and so on. As new projects are introduced, participants can access the intranet and browse the database for similar projects to get a good idea of what to expect. Participants can also contact people from old projects to get firsthand knowledge of what to expect in similar situations.

A real-life example of such a tool is the one used by a global consulting firm, McKinsey & Company. The system operates like a network structure where specialized information and insights generated from previous assignments across various industry and different geographic regions can be created, stored, and studied (McKinsey and Company, 1996).

Implementing the Knowledge Management System

Prior to implementation, the PMO must communicate any changes to the relevant project teams. Employees tend to be unwilling to share information if they expect that their work will not be acknowledged prior to its being distributed organizationwide. Because of such reasons, a discussion is necessary to obtain the support of all project participants to achieve a successful implementation. Key managers must communicate this message to all participants to obtain their commitment to actively participate in the knowledge-building process.

Knowledge Harvesting

As the oversight and management responsibilities of the PMO increase, so does the complexity of its knowledge management role. A point person may be required to collect and control the knowledge assets, building asset inventories aligned by portfolio or program. The point person is accountable for ensuring that all project documentation and supporting information is collected, collated, and stored, as well as for making sure that the organization's knowledge management process is operating as a best practice. One such method to achieve it is known as *knowledge harvesting* (Pugh and Dixon, 2008).

Knowledge harvesting is a highly interactive session to gain product knowledge from the community who owns it and those who maintain or build it. The process (explained in the next section) exposes all stakeholders to the intricacies and nuances of existing programs and gives them an improved understanding of how a product fits into a program and aligns them with the corporate objectives. Because the process is intended to be iterative, these sessions are repeated after a prescribed period to ensure that data is current and correct.

A Case for PMO: The PMO and Improving the Organization's Knowledge

Consider this question: Does your organization have subject matter experts (SMEs) who have become integral to your performance? Would their exit prove detrimental to your daily (and long-term) operations? The chances are the answer to these questions is yes. If that is the case, then knowledge management is for you because, if your SME walks out, you have somewhere to go to find out exactly what it was that he or she did every day.

And that's exactly what happened to FAS Inc. The organization saw a recognized financial accounting standards expert—let's call him Hal—deciding to move onto greener pastures. This person was the cornerstone of the FAS systems unit, and because the implementation of accounting standards is not everyone's idea of fun, he was left to deliver without any interference from his colleagues. When he left, there was not just a gap but a yawning chasm. Because Hal was the de facto expert, he rarely documented his work, instead relying on his knowledge to drive his projects. This worked well for the organization until Hal was gone. Then everyone realized that they were in a bit of a mess. Everyone was now left wondering, "Just what did Hal the SME expert do?" To make matters worse, a new version of the existing expensing application was required by the end of the quarter to report on stock option expenses for FAS's client base. And regardless of the SME loss, government regulations and business partners wait for no one. A gallant project team had taken on the assignment and worked long hours to determine how the current process worked, the state the new application was in (Hal had started it but his documentation was limited), and the effort required to complete it. Bottom line: missed deadlines, cost overruns, and a promise not to get caught out again made by senior management. They decided to spread the knowledge on financial accounting standards around the organization and concluded that knowledge management would be a good idea for their client services program (and all their other programs as well). They realized that, although an expense may be associated with setting the process up, it would pay off through faster product time to market, improved quality, improved training, and better team interaction.

After the project went live, the PMO management team went back to the drawing board to determine how to collect and manage their knowledge assets. They decided to do an electronic survey on their extended team to find out who was strong in which areas. The survey was filled out by each person and adjusted where appropriate by management (to account for modesty and perhaps ego). The results were correlated and then ranked to determine the experts in different areas. Based on this ranking, the knowledge management program was developed. The most vulnerable areas were addressed first, with those better served scheduled for later review. A knowledge hub was established and partitioned by area of expertise. A series of knowledge harvesting sessions was undertaken, with the results being used as the base to build the hub. Subject owners were appointed to collect all documentation and assets referenced in the harvest.

Based on the results of the SME Survey, FAS Inc. determined that the area where they were most vulnerable was expense reporting (ER). The PMO set up a harvest session to collect as much information as possible about the ER process and about the systems used to support it. Their first task was to set up a planning meeting with the key stakeholders for the subject. For this, they invited sponsors, customers, original project team members, and owners of several similar applications in the company. In the planning meeting the team was introduced to each other and to the harvest facilitator. They reviewed how the process would work and determine which areas would be covered in the harvest session. An agenda was created for the harvest session and distributed to the various parties. As the time approached, the stakeholders follow up with the invited participants to make sure they would attend.

It was clear at the outset of the session that many attendees were reluctant contributors, believing the effort to be a waste of time. The session kicked off, and the invited customers began to complain about the shortcomings of the process being harvested, creating some discomfort with the company attendees. The event facilitator explained that the goal of the event was to assist in building knowledge so as to improve the process for everyone. He then asked the customer to explain how the process worked from his point of view. His comments began the dialogue. Once the other stakeholders began to listen to the customers, they were able to contribute, and the atmosphere changed from one of polarization to one of cooperation, with all parties improving their understanding. At the end of the meeting, a harvesting document was created and sent out to all stakeholders. All involved agreed that the exercise had been very beneficial: the customers because they understood more about the process background and the company because they heard the customers' point of view.

With the harvest session completed, the PMO assigned a point person on the FAS team responsible for collecting the information to be placed in the hub. Armed with the minutes from the harvesting session, the point person—let's call him Steve—began the process of gathering the knowledge assets to add to the hub. The session minutes provided the contact information and location of those assets. Speaking further with those involved, Steve was able to complete the gathering process two weeks after the harvesting session. He returned the information to the PMO, who stored it based on predefined search criteria set up during the planning sessions: marketing information, business requirements, systems requirements, technical information, user feedback, client implementation instructions, etc. With the assets in place, the hub was launched.

The Harvesting Process

There are five distinct phases to the knowledge harvesting process: select, plan, capture, transfer, and reuse. The process starts by deciding what is to be reviewed, then a plan is drawn up to accomplish an analysis. It is then executed and the process is completed with the reuse of materials gathered as part of a training and education practice.

Phase 1: Selection

Deciding what information to harvest is based on the need of the organization. The need may be prompted by a project team's being disbanded at project completion, by their taking project knowledge with them, or by a contractor's leaving the company, taking the lessons he learned away from the company. Thus, before project development can commence, a complete review of the existing process may be required.

Phase 2: Planning the Harvest

A harvest requires the participation of two distinct groups: those who know, *the originators,* and those who seek to know, *the brokers.* The process is supported by a facilitator.

- *Originators* are those considered to be subject matter experts (SMEs) in the area to be reviewed. They can include original team members, those who manage a product or area, or those who understand the operation under review.

- *Brokers* are those who would benefit from the knowledge. They can be teams responsible for enhancements of a product, those undertaking a similar project, and others.

- *Facilitators* are those who chair the process and who will drive the questioning, assist with documenting the results, and ensure that session participants adhere to the harvesting rules.

Before the harvest can take place, the key stakeholders should be gathered together to discuss the format of the harvest and the goals. Areas to be harvested should be agreed on and documented as an agenda, which should be distributed in advance among the event participants, along with the guidelines for participation. Those participating as brokers should prepare questions that they think are relevant to the topic. Originators should gather together information: documents, manuals, process definitions, checklists, and whatever they feel is relevant to the exercise.

Phase 3: Data Capture

The harvest session is the primary method for capturing the information required for the library. It is a highly interactive brainstorming session that can take place across business units and locations. Tools such as video conferencing, web seminars, and other vehicles can be used for remote participants. The facilitator welcomes participants and explains the session's rules (e.g., no interrupting when another person is speaking, everyone must think outside the box, punctuality is a must, and so on) and the tools that will be used.

The facilitator will have a record of the discussions as they take place in the meeting, with follow-up sessions arranged should more detail be required. As each topic in the agenda is covered, the facilitator will work to draw information from the originators while trying to engage the brokers in questioning. Any documents or information referenced will be noted and collected after the meeting. The resulting notes will provide a valuable knowledge asset that can be used immediately to help with knowledge transfer between the originators and the brokers.

The harvesting session typically begins with the facilitator's having to drive the discussion. Many of those participating will not see the value at the outset of the conversation, especially because a time commitment is required. However, as the meeting moves forward, the attendees will begin to realize the advantage of such a gathering, rapport will develop, and creative juices will start to flow. The results can be measured both tangibly in terms of documentation and assets created and intangibly by the improvement of team dynamics and intrapersonal relationships.

Phase 4: Transfer of Knowledge

Once the harvesting session is complete, it will be necessary to return to some attendees to collect supporting information such as project stage deliverables, marketing information, and other documents. Once gathered, this data can be collated and stored in the knowledge hub in such a way that it is publishable and searchable. It should be available to all who would benefit or be interested in its use. Although anyone can be assigned this task, it is best to assign it to someone who has a vested interest in the creation of the hub, such as the program or project manager (or team member) responsible for a new project for which existing knowledge assets have yet to be collected.

Phase 5: Reuse It, Update It, Refresh It

Although the knowledge management team will be involved in the establishment of the various knowledge hubs, all interested parties should be responsible for ensuring that the information is fresh and up-to-date. The PMO should lead the efforts to make sure that the various project stakeholders responsible for the repository content will run it according to best practice (i.e., according to the benchmark in the industry) and mandate that the people who own the data must update the hub.

Conclusion

Formalized knowledge management is quickly being accepted as a best practice at many large corporations, because the value of centralized assets stored and the advantages to distributed project teams becomes increasingly apparent. Although there are drawbacks regarding the expense of enabling such a process—the investment in training and formalized methodologies (and possibly the need to purchase software and hardware to support the endeavor) will be required—there are many benefits, both tangible and intangible, which have been discussed in this chapter.

Once established, the knowledge management hub will facilitate expedited learning by all staff members, often providing a context for an undertaking that otherwise would be dependant on subject matter experts. The knowledge hub will also reduce centralized reliance on a limited number of individuals, thereby reducing the risk to ongoing operations resulting from staff turnover and limited resource availability. Meanwhile, new projects will benefit from a centralized repository that can help avoid missed requirements due to unknown product information, undocumented lessons learned, and missing project requirements and documentation from past iterations.

As with all best practices, good knowledge management requires the support of the senior management team. Advocates at a high level will assist with acceptance and success as the methods and processes are rolled out to the public at large.

5 Things You Need to Remember from This Chapter

1. The definition of knowledge management

2. The PMO's role in managing knowledge

3. The benefits, both tangible and intangible, offered by the PMO's knowledge management role to the organization

4. The process involved to set up PMO's knowledge management function (i.e., design the knowledge management hub, determine the suitable medium, and implement the system)

5. The steps in knowledge harvesting

Project Management Training

We have seen that the PMO is responsible for many complex processes that require expertise and skills to implement. Core to those responsibilities is the need to support and mentor good project management practices within the organization. Key to achieving that aim is a training program that supports the PMO stakeholders' needs at all levels. Thoughtful, relevant project management training is a major contributing factor to the success of the PMO and its community.

Training for success is not a new idea. Aristotle summed up the need for education and training more than two thousand years ago: "Excellence is an art won by training and habituation. We do not act rightly because we have virtue or excellence, but we rather have those because we have acted rightly. We are what we repeatedly do. Excellence, then, is not an act but a habit."* The ability to execute is not something that we are born with, unfortunately. At birth we know absolutely nothing. Not much has changed since Aristotle's day. We may have developed such marvels as the combustion engine, the computer, manned spaceflight, and so on, but,

---

*Aristotle, Greek critic, philosopher, physicist, and zoologist (384–322 BCE).

when we don't know them, the simplest actions still require major changes in brain activity to carry out (the use of a spoon is one such example).

The same applies to our ability to perform complex tasks in the workplace. As far as the authors are aware, no one has yet been born a project or program manager. They may have the aptitude, but hand them the tools without training, and all you will have is a collection of tools.

This chapter sets out the basics on what the PMO will need to know to facilitate successful project management training. It will review the requirements for all skill levels and suggest formats that will ensure targeted training that can build careers, improve morale, and help the PMO accomplish corporate goals.

Depending on the corporate culture, training programs to support the PMO may be easy or difficult to develop. Many large companies (such as Apple, Procter & Gamble, and IBM) place much importance on a well-educated workforce. They know that keeping employees up-to-date with the latest industry practices will boost morale and improve productivity. Some organizations, though, are not focused on training, and it may be left to the individual to find the education. One issue, however, will quickly become apparent with limited training: Without providing adequate training, it will be difficult for the PMO to educate the organization on project management matters, thus hindering its goals to add value to the organization. The following sections elaborate the reasons for providing project management training to the organization and offer suggestions on how to structure it best.

Reasons for Training

There are a number of reasons for encouraging training within an organization, such as the following ones.

Training for Competitive Advantage

Globalization has some positive results such as easier exchange of information and knowledge, as well as lower operating cost derived from outsourcing offshore. However, by the same token, globalization also creates a more competitive environment. As a result, every company needs to place a greater focus on quality service delivery in order to separate one business from the competition. In other words, project teams will be required to learn new skills and tools that can increase the company's product and service quality, while making the company's operation more efficient timewise and budgetwise.

Training for Acceptance

When best practices are introduced, training is a key step in gaining buy-in for the people involved. Courses should be tailored to suit all those whose daily roles interact with the PMO. They should cover the gamut of experience from an introduction to project management through intermediate level training and more complex certification (Six Sigma® or PMP®).

Many methods are available to facilitate training online: tutorials, webinars, digital media, taught courses, certification courses, university certification, and so on. Whatever process is selected, the goal should be to give those enrolled the tools to do well for the business, improving their skill sets and ability, at the same time improving their own prospects for career and personal growth. This, in turn, will allow employees to personally experience the benefits of having a PMO, which helps with the PMO's integration into the organization.

Training for Personal Growth

When developing training programs, the PMO should consider the desire of participants to enhance career prospects and mobility within the organization. There should be a well-mapped hierarchy that can be applied to progression through the company ranks.

For example, should a person want to move from a project manager position (i.e., someone who manages smaller projects with a few stakeholders within a department) to a senior project manager (whose endeavors run cross-department and often cross-organization and involve many stakeholders; see Chapter 19), it may be necessary for them to complete some form of project management certification. When possible, the training should be developed so that it can be credited against a more complex qualification. For instance, a Project Management Institute (PMI) certified course on risk management is worth a number of PMI Professional Development Units (PDU®), which can be used to help meet the qualification requirements for PMI's Project Management Professional (PMP®) designation. At the end of the day, when employees are willing to pursue a career within the organization, it will result in a lower employee turnover rate and improved staff quality. In other words, such training adds value to the organization's human resource management.

Training as a Morale Booster

A corporation's willingness to provide good training and education demonstrates commitment to the employees. It proves to team members that they are valued and worth investing in.

From the employees' perspective, they are generally very willing to learn and apply new skills that will produce visible, immediate results. Thus, investment in development will be paid off as turnover and on-boarding costs are reduced and productivity is increased, which will seep directly into the company's balance sheet. Generally, the most successful companies are those that invest heavily in training.

In some companies, the pursuit of project management training is closely tied to the organization's overall learning and development programs. For these companies, their professional development programs feature project management skills training as one of the bedrocks of staff development, with training that is open to all associates from entry level up. Considering all of these benefits, the PMO is challenged to work closely with various project offices, in addition to being a learning and development coordinator, to create a project management training program that is consistent with the organization's strategic business objectives.

Developing a Training Program That Works

When developing a program, consideration should be given to the ultimate objectives of the PMO: the management of projects to bring quantifiable benefits to the organization and help it achieve its goals. To do this, focus should be placed on project management training, including best practices, systems training, and knowledge management processes.

A good rule of thumb for training requirements is to look at the PMBOK *Guide to Project Management Knowledge Areas*. There are nine areas that they deem key to good project management, and the PMO fosters these best practices:

1. Integration management (the planning and execution of a project)

2. Scope management (extent of work)

3. Time management (task and duration estimation)

4. Project cost management (budgeting and estimates)

5. Quality management (quality assurance and control)

6. Human resource management (team development)

7. Communications management (planning, stakeholder administration)

8. Risk management (risk identification, analysis, and mitigation)

9. Procurement management (contracting, purchasing, and vendor management).

A good PMO training program should encompass these areas.*

There are multiple channels for executing training programs; e-learning, classroom, coaching, mentoring, and peer-to-peer are some examples. Each can be used to tailor training to a specific audience. Indeed, a combination of all methods is becoming more common within large organizations. E-learning is often used to prepare people for classroom-based courses with follow-up coaching and online sessions to supplant the knowledge gained.

Before a new training program can be implemented, the PMO must understand the project management capabilities of existing project offices and teams, so that the training materials can be directly applicable to the processes used in a project (i.e., budgeting and cost management, risk management, knowledge asset management, resource planning, and so on). If no formal training is in place, it is likely that many different methods are used across the organization to execute the same processes.

It is important that the program be flexible enough to deliver the range of education required to all stakeholders. Focus should be placed on project and program management–specific skills: risk management, project cost management, communications, knowledge management, motivation, team building, and so on. Generally, the course objectives should be quantifiable so that, upon completion, the exercise can be determined to be a success or not.

For example, PMP certification training for PMO project managers has a measurable objective: to provide the education required so that participants can become certified as a Project Management Professional (PMP). The course enhances project management skills and, in turn, the expertise of the PMO itself. Success can then be determined by the students' ability to pass the certification exam. The program itself may be complex and require much time to be invested, but its outcome, favorable or not, is determined immediately through the exam.

Of course, improvement in project management skills as a result

---

*As detailed in Project Management Institute, *A Guide to the Project Management Body of Knowledge (PMBOK® Guide)—Third Edition,* Project Management Institute, Inc., 2004. Copyright and all rights reserved. Material from this publication has been reproduced with the permission of PMI.

of taking the course may not be immediately apparent, but in time improvements in project metrics for those staff members should become visible.

PMO Training Structure Examples

Figure 9.1 shows a breakdown of an example PMO training program. There are three major programs: basic concepts, intermediate con-

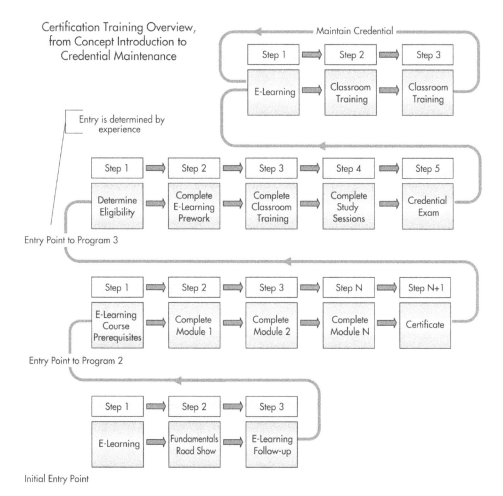

Figure 9.1 From entry to certification, how the PMO's training program progresses.

cepts, and advanced. The courses are designed with the audience's needs in mind. Generally, the completion of one program would be a prerequisite for enrollment in the next level. However, exceptions can be made based on an attendee's level of experience and knowledge. There is overlap in each area, but it can be assumed that all facilities offered in the lower-level option are available to the next program.

Let us apply the structure detailed in Figure 9.1 to a hypothetical situation at FAS Inc.: the introduction of a portfolio and program management (PPM) methodology (a centralized process to manage all aspects of a program such as resources, time, quality, risk, and so on) to drive the PMO's best practices for project management.

Program 1: Basic Concepts in Portfolio and Program Management (PPM)

The audience for this offering consists of those who have a peripheral interest in the systems and concepts being introduced. For example, for a developer who will enter hours worked in the billing section of a new program and portfolio management system, the introduction will give an overview of the role the developer plays in the planning and delivery of a project. The training sessions can be conducted in the following ways:

◻ *Online Offerings.* For those who are new to PPM or who will have very limited exposure, e-learning offers an excellent opportunity to familiarize themselves with the training concepts, terminology, and theories behind the PPM processes to be adopted by the PMO. It can also provide a handy reference for those seeking specific information in a particular area (completion of time entry, for example). This channel offers flexibility and is very cost-effective; it does not require absences from the workplace to complete.

- *Classroom Instruction Covering Project and Program Management Basics.* Classroom instruction enables attendees to see the processes in action and to pinpoint how their contribution will become part of the overall picture. Although this option is more costly than e-learning, it can assist in obtaining buy-in from peripheral stakeholders. Instruction can take the form of formal classes or of presentation in road shows, where an instructor delivers the material to various interested groups.

- *Coaching and Peer-to-Peer Interaction.* This very effective training method can be used to prepare, supplement, or enhance course material. A hands-on walk-through of the new process from a veteran or a review of the material with someone familiar with the processes involved can be vital in instilling knowledge.

Program 2: Intermediate PPM Concepts and Training

Aimed at those with a desire to build their skills in the PPM arena, Program 2 introduces project and program management concepts in detail to the attendee. It can also be used as a refresher course for people who are familiar with the processes but whose skill set may require updating. The course teaching should have the following criteria:

- *Classroom Instruction Covering All Aspects of Project Management.* The coursework presented in a classroom setting should be interactive, giving attendees the chance to practice some of the skills they are learning in a group setting. This will improve the chances of knowledge transfer and enhance the experience for the participant. It also facilitates peer-to-peer networking. Separate modules should be taught for each of the major project management knowledge areas. Instruction can be in-house (certified by the Project Management Institute) or provided by certified reputable vendors.

◘ *The Course Should Be University Accredited if Possible.* Many large corporations will work with local university business schools to deliver professional training. Courses underwritten by academic institutions give the attendee a real sense of achievement and can be used for future accreditation in the discipline being studied.

The coursework should lead to certification after a number of units have been completed. For example, an introduction to project management may feature modules on project time management, project risk management, project resource planning, project cost management, project quality management, project change management, and project planning. Completion of several of these modules should lead to a certificate. If possible, modules should be designed to be acceptable professional development units (PDUs)* for use with PMP certification.

Program 3: Advanced Concepts

Program 3 presents advanced concepts for study by the audience and will lead to completion of the training. This will require a time investment from both the company and the participants. Both the introductory and intermediate programs are prerequisite, although experience can be a substitute. The entry requirements for the advanced training should be strictly followed, thereby ensuring that the person has the correct experience and aptitude to complete the training.

As an example, if training is to be undertaken for the PMI PMP® certification, certain criteria must be met before beginning. For those with a bachelor's degree or equivalent, 4,500 hours of project man-

*The Project Management Institute's Project Management Professional certification. See www.pmi.org for more information.

agement experience are required, 7,500 for those without a degree. Because this experience will be verified by the PMI, it is worthwhile having the completion and validation of this information as a prerequisite for any training that will result in the PMP credential.

As with Program 2, where possible, the training should be attached to university-accredited coursework and should lead to professional certification. The instruction will be in-depth and will cover the topic in great detail. It will be complemented by extensive home study, with regular meetings to review and advise on coursework. The program should be as interactive as possible to maximize knowledge transfer.

Also at the advanced level, *coaching* is essential to success. Study groups with experienced course graduates should be offered as part of the course with attendance required. These should be used to review concepts and to assist those who may have struggled in class. The sessions can be at a person-to-person or group level and should give plenty of opportunity to practice skills learned in the classroom setting. Figure 9.1 shows conceptually how progress through each program will eventually lead to certification and credential maintenance.

Conclusion

Although the benefits of education and training are quantifiable, a cost is associated with the realization of those advantages. As with any operational efficiency undertaking, good training requires investment. It is important that the sponsors of your PMO understand this because they will have to advocate and fund the methods used. Expenses include opportunity cost (your staff will be at training, not at work), direct costs associated with those employees attending, the cost of instruction, and expenses associated with delivery (for instance, printed handouts, computer media, website access, and so on).

A Case for the PMO: Training

There are many reasons to attend training. It may be mandated, new processes may be introduced that require coaching, or it may be something you would like to learn to help you deliver on your job. We interviewed Kerry Murphy, one of FAS's project managers, and here is her account on the company's training, which had allowed her to choose courses suited to both her job and areas of interest.

I first became aware of project management as a discipline when I was asked to lead technical projects that included staff who were much more experienced than I was. Because I had no direct reports at the time, I decided to look into the training offerings that were available for project team motivation. This brought me in direct contact with our PMO for the first time. They recommended that I take a project management fundamentals course, which contained a module on team building and would also give me a good overview of the other areas of PMO's best practice. The program I enrolled in was run under the auspices of a local university business school and also offered PDUs toward the Project Management Institute's Project Management Professional designation (which I was unfamiliar with).

Our first exercise involved my viewing a toy car and reporting its description back to my assigned project team. They were to draw it based on my report, which was poor. I did not really consider what the team would need when making my notes. The completed drawing was a long way from the car that I had been presented with. I also realized that I had not really listened to the instructor before I had undertaken the task, which meant I was actually delivering the requirements in a way that would result in certain failure. This setback had a dual effect on me. First of all, I listened to the instructor for the rest of the week, and second, I discovered an interest in the project management discipline that I have cultivated ever since.

Completion of the fundamentals course led me to other, more in-depth classes offered by the PMO and eventually to the Project Management Professional certification offered by the Project Management Institute. The net result of my PMO-sponsored training (which is ongoing) has been to improve my project management skills (I think I have come some distance since the toy car experience), to keep me up-to-date with changes within the discipline, and to enhance my opportunities within the company.

Employee training will require a major commitment from the PMO and the company's senior executive team. For a new PMO's best practices to gain acceptance, a training program that will address the needs of all stakeholders is required. Attention should be paid to the experience of the attendees, their role within the larger project management process, and their career focus. The structures put in place should give people opportunities to enhance their mobility prospects within the organization and build on their skill sets. A good training program will bring many advantages to the sponsoring company and will benefit the PMO. Staff will expand their project management skills, leading to improved performance on the job and ultimately to higher productivity and an improved bottom line.

5 Things You Need to Remember from This Chapter

1. Quality project management training is the foundation on which the PMO is built. It ensures that best practices are accepted and that stakeholders understand why and how they are applied.

2. Training should be relevant to responsibilities.

3. Completion of one training level should act as an entry point to the next.

4. When possible, training should lead to a recognized quali-fication; this will improve morale and lead to acceptance.

5. Willingness to invest in training demonstrates to your em-ployees that they are valued.

Project Resource Management

The success of an organization largely depends on the clever use of its unique resources. Ranging from staff, space, and intellectual property to funding, each resource is an asset to the organization. Because individual resources alone cannot create competitive advantage, organizations must learn how to integrate them to derive their optimum use through synergy. In this chapter, we will look at how companies can do that. We will start with an overview of what resource management is, followed by a discussion on the role of the PMO in managing project resources.

An Overview of Resource Management

Resources are basically the inputs that firms use to develop goods and services for customers, and they can be tangible or intangible in nature. *Tangible resources* are physical assets (e.g., buildings, machinery, computers, and other equipment). *Intangible resources* (e.g., brand names, trademarks, technology, and knowledge) are more difficult to evaluate, but they are no less valuable to the firm.

The impact of combined resources can vary depending on various factors, such as the organization's culture, the staff's personalities and thus their ability to work together in a team, the managers' style, and so on. For example, resources may flow fluidly from one project to another in an organization whose culture is open to sharing, whereas in a silo organization there is lack of communication and cooperation among the business units and therefore possible competition for resources. Looking at all these factors, it is clear that there ought to be a process to manage the various types of resources.

The PMO's Resource Management Role

Robert Grant, in his book *Contemporary Strategy Analysis* (2008), offers a simple approach to resource management for a company in three simple steps:

- *Step 1* is identifying the organization's key resources and their capabilities. The company first needs to look at what it does and what its main products and services are before identifying the resources that contribute the most.

- *Step 2* involves appraising the resources against two criteria. First, how important the resources are for generating sustainable competitive advantage; second, how strong or weak these resources are compared with competitors'.

- *Step 3* involves developing the strategy implications of step 1 and 2 above. Basically, this means finding out the most effective way to deploy the resources with the goal of achieving superior results for the company.

So how do these steps relate to the PMO's role? Resource management (i.e., the management of project staff, space, and other project equipment) is an important element in project management. The main aim of the resource management functionality of the PMO is an optimized use that creates competitive advantage for the company. In collaboration with project managers and the HR department, PMO's resource management functionality covers the following aspects:

- Providing resources
- Establishing resource management guidelines
- Forecasting future resource requirements

Providing Resources

PMO's strategic role in providing resources revolves around assisting project managers in project resource selection and engagement. For example, when looking at candidates for project team members' positions, such a review will consider their skills, experience, knowledge, and understanding of the organization's business practice. In most projects, there are three diferent types of personnel resources:

1. Project management resources (project managers, project support officers, project finance analyst, and so on)
2. Technical resources (subject matter experts)
3. Support resources (such as those from the IT and finance departments)

It is the responsibility of the PMO to ensure the availability of qualified resources, either internally or by obtaining resources external to the organization.

The process of fulfilling resource requirements should include the following steps:

- Project managers or project initiators submit a project resource request to the PMO for review.

- The PMO considers the available pool of skilled resources. In consultation with the project manager, the PMO dispatches the suitable staff into the projects.

- If an internal resource pool is not sufficient, the PMO will liaise with human resources (HR) to recruit more resources.

Establishing Resource Management Guidelines

Monitoring resource assignment and performance is an important part of the PMO's responsibility. To achieve an efficient resource management, the PMO must create standard guidelines for the following:

- Resource selection

- Resource acquisition

- Resource engagement

- Resource performance review (to be tied in closely with the rest of the organization's performance review method)

- Resource dispersal (for individual departures and at project completion)

Those guidelines are best developed in collaboration with project managers and the HR department to ensure that all parties' perspectives on resource management are taken into consideration and thus achieve their support.

Forecasting Future Resource Requirements

The PMO adds value to resource management by providing ongoing monitoring of the current resource utilization. Having comprehensive information on the overall resource assignments allows the PMO to understand the adequacy of current project resources and to determine the number of resources needed for future projects. Comparing current resource usage and future requirements, the PMO should be able to identify the gap and advise senior management of the necessary acquisition or dispersal.

A Case for the PMO: Resource Management

Hamel and Prahalad (1994) suggest that the size of the firm's resource is not the key determinant of capability. Rather, it is the firm's ability to leverage its resources that is important. Resources can be leveraged in the following ways:

1. *Concentrate resources* by focusing the available resources on projects whose outcomes will have the maximum impacts on the company's bottom line.

2. *Accumulating resources* through staff training and borrowing from other firms through cooperative arrangements, such as alliances and outsourcing.

3. *Complementing resources* by linking the resources with other complementary resources, which can generate greater effectiveness. For example, by putting product development staff, marketing staff, and accounting staff on the same team, the final product will satisfy the market requirement and stay within the company's budget.

4. *Conserving resources* by maximizing the utilization of resources. This can be done, for example, by reusing the same equipment on a number of projects through the end of the equipment's life span.

FAS Inc. discovered that a major challenge in the *matrix structure* introduced by the PMO was the allocation of human resources to development projects. Their project portfolio often had a dozen or more initiatives underway simultaneously that require upward of 20 people. Often those requested were the same folks—generally experts and top performers—with newer, less experienced people left on the bench. This created two problems: burnout among the senior staff and low morale in the junior team members. This always leads to interesting planning meetings. Some project managers wonder where everyone had gone because they found it impossible to get people to work on their deliverables, whereas other managers were famous for their ability to assign all resources to their project. The PMO also discovered that there was a tendency for functional managers with project management responsibilities to hold onto their own direct subordinates, even if they didn't really have the expertise to execute in the specific area. The lack of availability of those resources often led to delays in other projects, and a kind of deadlock ensued. Paul Witten, the PMO manager, and his team understood that for the PMO to execute successfully, the resource allocation process would have to be improved. To address the problem, a weekly resource planning meeting was convened by the PMO for each business unit. During the meeting, the various project managers request resources. At the end of the week, when all requests were placed, the PMO reviewed and allocated resources in a manner that made the best use of each person's time. The PMO staff considered project risks and project status (e.g., if one project was late and another completed ahead of schedule, then resources may be shifted from one project to the other) and tried wherever possible to "smooth or level" the resource requirements of the organization to avoid under- or overutilization "spikes."

Resource Scheduling

In large organizations, trying to manage numerous project staff can be very challenging that it may require in-depth mathematical analysis in order to find the most optimum use of each resource across the organization. Although this process can be complex, the basic concept, which basically involves moving resources around a number of projects' schedule (resource scheduling), is simple, as il-

Business Analyst Requirement

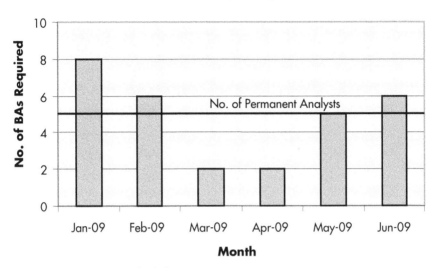

Figure 10.1 Resource scheduling.

lustrated by Figure 10.1. A PMO manager is trying to estimate whether the existing number of business analysts (BAs) is sufficient for the next six months. Currently, five analysts are working on a number of different projects. Based on the number of business proposals approved, there will be three more projects with fluctuating needs for analysts over the next six months, as summarized in the following table:

Resource Requirement—Business Analysts

	Jan-09	Feb-09	Mar-09	Apr-09	May-09	Jun-09
No. of BAs Required	8	6	2	2	5	6

Based on the graph in the figure, and in collaboration with the HR department, project managers, and senior managers, the PMO may suggest the following:

▢ Engage three external contractors on a short-term contract for the month of January. The pursuit of this alternative really depends on the organization's capability because such a solution may not be practical for every organization. Note how this solution involves job advertising, creating a contract, and so on. Another solution to fulfill resource shortages may involve postponing project activities (the impact on business caused by such action must be conducted prior to taking this action) or borrowing resources from other projects.

- Three of the onboard business analysts could be reassigned to nonproject work during the months of March and April because the drop in resource requirements is only temporary.

- Based on the forecast analysis, firing and rehiring the staff may not be a suitable option in this case since the "downtime" for the "excess resource" is manageable.

From this example, it is obvious that the aim of resource scheduling is to determine a fixed amount of resource that is sustainable over a long period of time. This exercise is aimed at optimizing the productivity of available resources while minimizing the amount of administrative work associated with hiring and firing (which may also result in the company's losing a qualified worker). In its application, resource scheduling must be carried out concurrently with the organization human resource policy.

Conclusion

Resource management can be an exhaustive exercise. In most cases, the complexity of the process can be handled by the available advanced methodology and sophisticated software to achieve an optimum resource management. However, at the end of the day, it is commitment from all of the parties involved that makes projects successful.

5 Things You Need to Remember from This Chapter

1. The purpose of resource management in an organization

2. The importance of understanding both the tangible and intangible resources needed in most of the projects run in your company

3. The resource management roles of PMO (e.g., help to provide resources to projects, establish resource management guidelines, forecast future resource requirements)

4. How to leverage resources

5. How to carry out resource scheduling

PART III

PROCESSES

Project Selection

A dynamic organization, in which people constantly come up with initiatives, is frequently confronted with numerous project proposals. The constraints on available resources make it crucial that every project selected supports the organization's goals. This prompts the need for a project selection process. Such a systematic process involves evaluating individual project proposals, allowing senior management to decide which projects would be best to invest its capital in so the organization can achieve its strategic goals. This is where the PMO comes into play.

In this chapter, we will discuss the PMO's role in ensuring that the projects selected will benefit the organization. As a part of its responsibility, the PMO creates the selection model and implements it. With this in mind, we will look at a number of factors to consider in developing the selection model. We will then present one model as an application example.

The Need for Project Selection

Which product to develop? Which market to expand? Which company to acquire? Faced with these competing alternatives, senior management needs a tool to assist in making the best decision. Each of these proposals has different costs, risks, and benefits. To make matters more complicated, rarely are those factors easily quantifiable. Thus, the aim of the project selection process is to achieve the greatest benefit for the organization that comes with the best allocation of resources and capital investment.

How to Select the Projects

Several techniques can be adopted to help senior management in selecting the right projects. To arrive at the most appropriate model, the organization needs to establish the following factors:

1. The organization's strategic goals
2. The project selection model

Establishing the Organization's Strategic Goals

Strategies are developed to meet specific objectives that allow a company to focus on growth and to compete more effectively against competitors. Within these objectives and strategic plans, projects must be selected and prioritized. The purpose of the projects should be to assist the company in effectively executing its strategies.

As part of its strategic advancement, every organization needs to generate a list of concrete objectives that will take them closer to fulfilling its mission and vision. Such a list should be specific. Thus, rather than producing a general and vague series of clichés about maximizing the bottom line, the items should be as specific as, for example, "Expanding the clothing range in the European market," "Reduce the fabric supply cost by 20 percent," or "Increase brand exposure to people in the 18–25 age group." By having a list of definite objectives, senior management can compare the organization's plan with the projects proposed before deciding which projects should go ahead.

The Project Selection Model

Considering the fact that not all project information can be boiled down to a 100 percent specific level, choosing one or more projects from a vast amount of proposals is a complex process. To deal with this problem, a decision-aiding model is necessary. Such models are helpful because they represent the problem's structure by extracting reality from the abstract issues. The more factors (and thus uncertainties) there are to consider, the more complex the model becomes.

The selection model will have to make some assumptions about the internal and external factors related to the organization. These estimates should be made while keeping in mind the reality of the situation the company faces. When choosing a selection model, the following three main characteristics should be taken into consideration:

1. *Realism.* The model should reflect as much "reality" as possible. For example, it should take into account the amount of capital, human resources, and technical capacity available to the company. It should also present a realistic expectation of the degree of risks associated with the projects.

2. *User-Friendliness.* The model should be simple enough for the decision makers to understand and flexible enough to modify as the organization's condition changes. By trying to make the model simple, though, the designers should not exclude relevant and important factors. In other words, they have to weigh the needs for comprehensiveness and practicality.

3. *Cost Efficiency.* The model must balance the preceding two characteristics. It must be sufficiently comprehensive to include all the necessary data (in order to make the selection process as realistic as possible), yet the cost involved in doing so (i.e., for data gathering, data analysis, and so on) must also be in proportion to the benefits that the project offers.

The Basic Types of a Project Selection Model

The PMO can use a number of techniques to evaluate projects. The technique that we propose here utilizes weighted criteria in the selection process. Using this method, business activities are weighed based on criteria that go beyond financial measures. Criteria such as those relating to customers, shareholders, the organization's business processes, and staff growth should be included in assessing a project's alignment with the vision and strategy of the organization.

Building on that concept, we can then assign weights to the criteria. We can adopt two types of weights: non-numeric (qualitative) and numeric (quantitative).

- The *qualitative* model is subjective. For example, projects may be categorized into qualitative criteria such as Poor, Good, and Excellent. A project may then be accepted if it lies above the boundary line that separates Poor and Good or rejected if it is considered Poor.

  Such subjectivity exposes the model to criticism because of its vagueness. As a result, the consensus on the correct status of a proposal will be the subject of long discussions among the members of senior management. However, it should be emphasized that the simplicity of a qualitative model does not mean that it is unreliable. On the contrary, such a model could be the most appropriate one for the organization, depending on the size and nature of the project and the organization itself. For example, the decision to select a small project would probably go faster with qualitative measures instead of pouring time and money into trying to quantify every single criterion.

- The *quantitative* model, on the other hand, assigns numbers to the criteria, in the hope that it presents more certainties in selecting one project over another. The construction of a qualitative model involves the selection of criteria and the

A Case for PMO: The PMO and Project Selection

It was another quarterly budget meeting at FAS Inc. Both senior project managers, Bill Clements and Kerry Murphy, were involved in an intense discussion with Mike O'Malley, the CFO, and Dea Chan, the head of the marketing department. For the next quarter, the IT department would get only $500,000 in their budget. This means that they could take on only one project: either Mike's, developing customized software for his finance department, or Dea's, an online platform for a product that FAS will launch soon. Mike's argument went like this: "If you make me this software, my staff can save a lot of time because they won't have to process payments to vendors manually ever again. Remember, this organization deals with one hundred and thirty-four vendors! With this software, my staff won't need to work long hours at the end of every month, and we wouldn't have to pay them overtime anymore." But Dea then chimed in: "Are you kidding me, Mike? Your staff can work a few more hours. We need this platform; otherwise the product won't sell! And *that* will cost the company money."

CEO Dave Strassen, who had been listening for a while, broke his silence: "Okay, the way I see it, we will have to prioritize one of these projects." Kerry Murphy suggested that, with Dave's input, they could start building a simple model to help with the decision making. They listed the criteria for what is important for FAS. They came up with three criteria: money was on top of the list (either money saved from not paying overtime or money gained from the new products selling very well). The other two criteria were employees' work-life balance (happier employees will stay with the company longer) and customers' satisfaction (the online platform will provide a lot of convenience for customers). The arguments on how to weigh each criterion went on and on for almost 40 minutes before Dave finally asked Dea and Mike to come up with a detailed analysis of how much money the company can save from Mike's project and how much money the company can gain from Dea's project. In addition, Bill and Kerry, as PMO representatives, were asked to provide an independent opinion on how much the other two criteria should be weighted. The PMO then conducted interviews with Mike's employees and the HR department, and reviewed some customer survey results on the product that's about to be launched before assigning the weights.

A week later, they had another meeting. The model yielded a result that says they should go with Dea's project. Dave looked over the report and agreed with it. After another 40 minutes of discussion, Dea agreed that, although the model favored her project, like it or not, the measures were still subjective. She decided to reduce the scope of her project so the IT department could start Mike's project in this quarter instead of the next. Dave had no objection. So, although a bit disgruntled at the beginning, Mike was just glad that his project finally got the go-ahead.

---

assignment of scores on the criteria (explained in more detail in this chapter).

Establishing the Project Selection Model

Before a selection model can be established, senior management must first list the factors that influence decision making. For example, if the projects propose the development of Product A rather than Product B, then the selection factors may include appearance, production cost, sale price, projected sales number, and related factors. The idea of having an exhaustive list must never be put aside. However, you must always be aware that such lists may complicate the selection process unnecessarily if a group of selected top five most influential factors is sufficient.

Once the list has been developed, two tasks remain. First, senior management has to decide on and number the factors in the order of their importance (i.e., which is first, second, third, fourth, and so on). For example, if management believes that the net present value (NPV) of profit produced by a certain product is more important than having that product penetrating a whole new market, then they might want to assign a higher score to the NPV factor and a lower score to the market penetration factor.

Given Factor X is more important than Factor Y, the next question is, "How much more important?" When confronted with that question, senior management has the option of assigning weights to the options. Generally, the sum of the weights of all factors should add up to one. In other words, this requirement reflects the contribution portion of one factor compared to the overall contribution of all the factors. The weight of each factor is to be multiplied by the assigned weight in order to obtain the overall score for the project prior to ranking the candidate projects.

Let's look at an example of how to apply the principle. The senior management of Company XYZ has to decide which product development project (A, B, or C) is the best investment for them. Before ranking the project, Company XYZ sets up selection criteria (refer to Table 11.1): The product must produce profit at least in the next three years, give advantage to the company in terms of controlling the market size, and must have a low long-term expenditure associated with customer support.

Separate scores are then assigned to distinguish various projected performance levels for the criteria. In this example, a higher score is adopted to indicate a more favorable performance (i.e., a product that produces $400,000 profit will be assigned a higher score than a product that produces $100,000 profit).

Another criterion has different importance to the company, prompting senior management to assign various weights to it. In the table, 3-Year Profit Projection is deemed to be the most important and

Table 11.1 Project Selection Example

Product Development Selection

			Score		
Criteria	1	2	3	4	5
3-year profit projection	< $50,000	$50,000–$150,000	$150,000–$300,000	$300,000–$500,000	$500,000<
Market size control	<10%	10%–20%	20%–50%	50%–70%	70%<
Customer support cost	$80,000	$60,000–$80,000	$40,000–$60,000	$20,000–$40,000	$20,000 >

Product Scores

Alternatives	3-Year Profit Projection (Weight: 0.5)	Market Size Control (Weight: 0.2)	Customer Support Cost (Weight: 0.3)	Total Score	Rank
Product A	5 × 0.5 = 2.5	1 × 0.2 = 0.2	2 × 0.3 = 0.6	3.3	1
Product B	1 × 0.5 = 0.5	2 × 0.2 = 0.4	4 × 0.3 = 1.2	2.1	2
Product C	2 × 0.5 = 1.0	5 × 0.2 = 1.0	3 × 0.3 = 0.9	2.9	3

is thus assigned the most weight, followed by Customer Support Cost and Market Size Control. In practice, there are various ways to determine the most appropriate number to reflect the weight. Such a technique, which involves extensive data gathering and complicated computerized formulas and models, is beyond the scope of this book.

For each product, its scores across the various criteria are multiplied by the assigned weights, producing a total score. The projects are then ranked, with the highest scored at the top.

Conclusion

Always bear in mind that models can churn out numbers and add more conviction to the argument. Whether highly quantitative or qualitative, models are decision-making aids. They can help crystallize a viewpoint or an argument. However, at the end of the day, the decision lies in the hands of people, not a model.

5 Things You Need to Remember from This Chapter

1. Know your organization's goals.

2. Use a methodical process in selecting projects to make sure they're aligned with your company's strategy.

3. Know the different characteristics to consider when developing a selection model that is suitable for your organization.

4. Understand the qualitative and quantitative methods, and when to use them.

5. Include nonmonetary criteria in the model.

Controlling Project Progress

In the previous chapter, we discussed the PMO's role in project selection. However, the PMO's role doesn't end there. Now that we have our projects lined up, the PMO will still be playing an important role in making sure that every project achieves its desired goals. In this chapter, we will discuss how the PMO can accomplish that through a series of *gateway reviews*.

The United Kingdom's Office of Government Commerce promotes the gateway process as a method to examine projects at key decision points in their life cycle before they are allowed to progress. The purpose of this process is twofold: first, to provide assurance that the projects can progress successfully to the next stage; second, to ensure that all projects are reviewed consistently by the same standard. One of the PMO's tasks will be to develop a gateway process that best suits their company. In this chapter, we will show how your PMO can do that.

Why Use a Gateway Review?

A gateway review examines the readiness of a project to proceed to the next stage. It allows the progressive commitment of resources while ensuring an accurate cost, benefits, and risk assessment. In other words, a gateway review is a way to ensure that:

- All project milestones and their deliverables have been accomplished.

- All skilled personnel and vendors or contractors are available to commence work.

- All other resources (facilities, space, and so on) are available for the next stage.

- The necessary budget to proceed to the next stage has been approved.

- Approval to proceed has been sought and given by the project sponsor and/or other appropriate authorities.

Making a Case for PMO: The PMO and Staged Reviews

FAS Inc. was faced with a complex project of massive proportion: automating business processes and supporting functions (e.g., accounts payable, accounts receivable, and setup of contracts) for Sarbanes-Oxley compliance. To complete the project, their first step was to identify which areas of the company are responsible for the financial reporting and the IT system they use. They also had to determine how financial data flows from those areas were to be finally captured in the financial reports. Understanding the scale of the project, Dave, the CEO, wanted a direct report on project progress. He assigned project leadership to someone from outside the company: a project manager named James Tobin, a financial expert with extensive IT experience. He would be assisted by a project team consisting of a senior technical staff from the IT department and another senior staff from the finance department. Because of its magnitude, the project was divided into eight subprojects that would look at how the financial data was processed in the different operational divisions of the company. Each subteam would also be led by a project manager and two staff (one each from the IT and finance departments).

It wasn't long before chaos reigned. James Tobin spent most of his time putting out fires instead of planning the next step of the project. Each subproject had different levels of complexities, which were due to the different size of each division and its varying ways of doing things. As a result, all of the eight subprojects moved at a different pace, and James had trouble keeping up with what each subproject was up to. He had no control over the differing quality of each subproject's deliverables.

James Tobin sensed that, unless he could bring all these subprojects to move in unison, it really would be like herding cats for the rest of the project. (And it was going to be a long project!) So he consulted the PMO and Kerry Murphy, a senior project manager at the PMO, suggesting that he use the gateway review. The gateway review subjected all the subprojects to the same monitor and control standards. Once James understood how it works, he asked the PMO to give an induction to explain to the project managers how the gateway review works. James also informed the project managers that, from that point onward, all of them would be given the same deadlines reflecting the different stages in the review. And that finally brought all the subprojects to move forward in synch. James was then ready to move the project to the next stage.

Of course, the case study above is an oversimplification of what really happened, but the moral of the story is how a PMO tool, the gateway review, can be used to improve projects' quality assurance.

The Different Stages in the Gateway Review

The review is commonly divided into five distinctive parts*:

1. Gate 1: Concept

2. Gate 2: Design

3. Gate 3: Development

4. Gate 4: Implementation

5. Gate 5: Finalization

However, it is perfectly alright for an organization to end up with different gates, depending on the nature of its projects.

Gate 1: Concept

Objectives: The concept phase is the first formal period in the project life cycle. It allows a business initiative to be reviewed in order to ensure that the idea is feasible (technically and financially) and beneficial enough for the organization to make the investment. In other words, the concept phase ensures that any idea makes business sense.

Deliverables: Business Case

Activities:

▶ Document the high-level description of the concept and obtain approval from the relevant business unit's manager.

▶ Verify the concept's alignment with the organization's strategy.

▶ Develop an indicative timeframe and quantify the amount of financial commitment and resources necessary to complete the overall project.

---

*Adapted from the United Kingdom's Office of Government Commerce "Gateway Review for Programmes and Projects."

➤ Identify relevant risks and issues.

➤ Identify the parties impacted by the concept.

➤ Provide other relevant information to assist the organization's executives with decision making.

➤ Attach a Cost-Benefit Analysis to the business case.

The PMO's task is to gather the business cases from various business units and bring them forward for review by the organization's executive. As a part of this task, the PMO has the obligation to review the business case to ensure that it contains all the necessary information for review by the project committee.

Gate 2: Design

Objectives: Once a business case has been reviewed and approved by the committee, the concept has gained formal recognition. In the design phase, the business case will evolve into a project plan, which provides a more detailed understanding of the project's approach and its requirements (resources, schedules, deliverables, risks, and the impacts involved) to take the project forward. In this phase, the detailed functional and technical designs for the project are also developed.

Deliverables: Project Plan

Activities:

➤ Define the number of staff required for the project and allocate the resources there; consider external resources if internal resources are not sufficient.

➤ Define project scope and its deliverables; establish a clear boundary between what is in scope and what is out of scope.

➤ Develop a detailed breakdown of each activity required to complete the project, which is necessary to derive a more accurate estimate of project schedule and costing (i.e., a more accurate estimate can be derived from "buying 2 gallons of white paint and hiring a painter for 13 hours" than from "paint the bedrooms").

➤ Identify the project's sponsor and appropriate funding source.

- ▶ Refine the project's risks (and their mitigation plans), cost estimates, and project's impacts based on the organization's structure and operation.
- ▶ Achieve approval and work commitment from all the stakeholders involved.
- ▶ Identify and review various alternatives for project delivery with a recommendation of the preferred approach.
- ▶ Develop detailed functional and technical designs.
- ▶ Define project reporting requirements and project management practices to be applied in the next stage.
- ▶ Establish a central repository for project documents.

Gate 3: Development

Objectives: Once the project plan has been reviewed and approved by the committee, it is authorized to proceed to the development phase. Here, products are built according to what is outlined in the designs.

Deliverables: Project's Products
At this stage, multiple approvals may be needed for multiple deliverables, and approvals may also be required for project variations in the event of a change of scope or an increase in the project cost or duration.

Activities:

- ▶ Develop and test products.
- ▶ Develop implementation strategy.
- ▶ Develop more accurate cost, schedule, and resource estimate for the next stage.
- ▶ Construct (build) once products have been coded and tested.

Gate 4: Implementation

Objectives: The purpose of this phase is to ensure that the project's deliverables are implemented to the appropriate environment.

Deliverables: Implemented products running smoothly as a part of the business's operation.

Activities:

▶ Communicate with stakeholders to determine the most appropriate time to carry out the implementation.

▶ Implement the deliverables, if required, in a number of releases.

▶ Conduct customer review to ensure that every glitch can be identified and fixed.

Gate 5: Finalization

Objectives: This last stage is incorporated into the gateway process to ensure that all projects are properly closed with an appropriate review and handed over to the staff who will operate it or be in charge of it on a day-to-day basis. (With some projects, the people who were involved in developing the product will not oversee it in the long run once it is integrated into the company's operation.)

Activities:

▶ Ensure that all deliverables' components have been implemented properly.

▶ Ensure that the operation of all deliverables has been properly handed over to the appropriate business unit personnel.

▶ Obtain sign-offs from project sponsor and other stakeholders.

▶ Inform project team members and stakeholders about the formal closing of the project.

▶ Transfer relevant documents from the project's repository into the PMO's knowledge management system database.

▶ Conduct a postimplementation review on project performance, which may be conducted by PMO personnel instead of project staff, and pass the result on to the project committee.

Deliverables: Postimplementation Review

Gateway Review Tools

The PMO's use of the gateway review can be supported by a number of available tools, such as the following:

◻ *Gateway Review Summary Diagram.* A summary diagram, like the one in Figure 12.1, shows a high-level view of the stage the project is in and the roles of each project participant throughout the project's life cycle.

◻ *Gateway Review Checklist.* A comprehensive checklist, such as the one shown in Figure 12.2, may be used in connection with the Gateway Review Summary Diagram. The checklist should be done according to the gating sequence, and it should also be specific enough, listing all of the detailed level activities.

Conclusion

In this chapter, we discussed the PMO's micromanagerial role in ensuring periodically that every project is ready before it goes any further. The adoption of formal checkpoints in a gateway review encourages an effective and efficient project delivery, thus improving the probability of its success. In the next chapter, we will look at the PMO's macromanagement of projects at a program level.

(text continues on page 143)

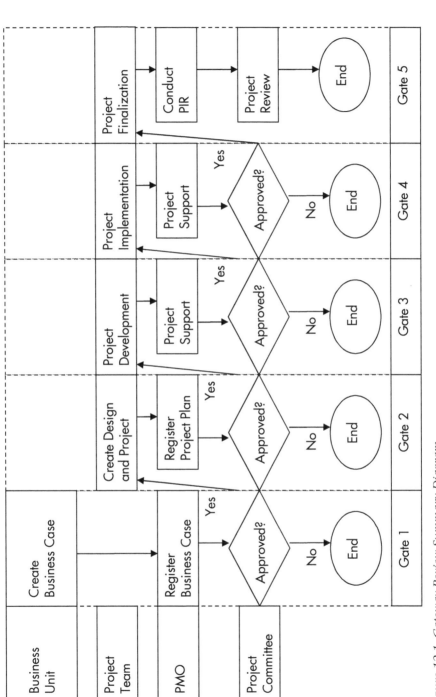

Figure 12.1 Gateway Review Summary Diagram.

Gate 1: Concept	
Describe project scope	☐
Estimate how long the project will take	☐
Identify risks and issues	☐
Align concept with organization's strategy	☐
Conduct Cost-Benefit Analysis	☐
Create a business case	☐
Obtain the necessary approvals prior to submission	☐
Gate 2: Design	
Define project scope	☐
Identify project sponsor	☐
Identify project participants	☐
Refine project's risks and issues	☐
Develop functional and technical design	☐
Create a project plan	☐
Obtain the necessary approvals prior to submission	☐
Gate 3: Development	
Test products	☐
Document users' experience	☐
Plan product's implementation	☐
Obtain the necessary approvals prior to product delivery to client	☐

Figure 12.2 Gateway Review Checklist.

Gate 4: Implementation	
Communicate implementation plan to parties that will be affected	☐
Plan the implementation in a number of releases	☐
Seek feedback from users at the end of each release	☐
Obtain the necessary approvals prior to implementation	☐
Gate 5: Finalization	
Review feedback after implementation	☐
Carry out any necessary changes prior to finalization	☐
Obtain sign-offs	☐
Close project	☐
Conduct postimplementation review	☐

Figure 12.2 Gateway Review Checklist. (continued)

5 Things You Need to Remember from This Chapter

1. The purpose of gateway review as an instrument to measure projects' readiness to advance to the next stage

2. The different stages commonly included in the gateway review

3. What each project has to deliver at the different stages

4. The importance of identifying the staff to cooperate to obtain approval to proceed to the next stage

5. The different tools that can be used in the gateway review (e.g., a Gateway Review Summary Diagram and a Gateway Review Checklist)

Program Monitoring and Control

In the last chapter, we discussed the PMO's micromanagerial role. In this chapter, we will discuss a role that is no less important: macro-managing the projects at the program level, where the PMO is to provide a snapshot of the program as a whole as opposed to on a piecemeal basis (i.e., at project level). Managing a program is an iterative process of collecting the required information, analyzing it, reporting it to the business executives who will then take any control measures necessary, and then going back to monitoring the program. We will review the tools useful for the PMO in each of these steps.

The key function for the tools is to provide crucial information to project managers, program managers, project committees, and other project participants with relevant information regarding ongoing projects, which is vital for them to have in order to stay informed and make timely decisions.

The Monitoring Process

A typical program monitoring process involves the activities shown in Figure 13.1.

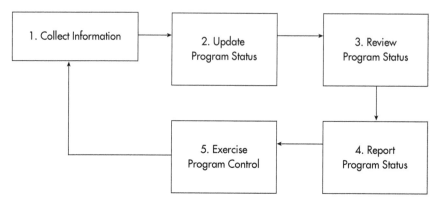

Figure 13.1 Steps in program monitoring.

1. Information Collection

Information, such as each project's total expenditure to date, its completion status to date, and so on, is collected through a project status report (refer to Chapter 7), which has to be done by each project office with an agreed-on frequency. The project status report provides key information about the different activities to be performed in a project and shows how well those activities are progressing when compared to the plans. This type of information has to be collected periodically to offer the necessary data for the PMO to do its monitoring and control tasks.

2. Program Status Update

Upon receiving the information, the PMO analyst updates the program repository, which is basically a collection of projects' statuses. The purpose of such a repository is to provide an overview of the actual progress of each project compared to its schedule and to other projects. In creating the repository, these are the most important aspects that need to be included:

◻ Actual percentage of project completed versus planned completion

◘ Actual expenditure versus planned expenditure

◘ Actual budget versus planned budget

◘ Actual time spent versus planned schedule

A sample template for the repository is shown in Figure 13.2.

These days, software is available to help the organization in monitoring its projects (refer to Chapter 15 for a more in-depth discussion on PMO system selection). Selecting the best software for the company depends on a number of aspects, such as software capabilities, purchase price, system requirements, technical supports, and so on. Any software chosen must be able to act as a program repository.

3. Program Status Review

Once the PMO updates the repository, its next task is to analyze the status of those projects using the following metrics, before presenting them to the project steering committee.

Project Performance Metrics

We define metrics as a performance measurement tool. Metrics provide guidance on how the project performs against the initial plan in terms of schedule, time, and resources. The application of metrics in a project environment has a variety of uses, such as the following:

◘ Establishing consistent oversight of project performance in terms of cost, schedule, and resource utilization

◘ Facilitating comparison with industry standards for compliance purposes

◘ Facilitating industry benchmarking for the organization's project competency and capability

For the Financial Year: 2009/2010

Date: _____

Rank	Project Name	Completion		Budget		Expenditure		Verification	Escalation
		Planned Completion	Actual Completion	Planned Budget	Actual Budget	Planned Expenditure	Actual Expenditure	Number of Verification Requested	Issues / Risks / Changes to be resolved
1	ABC	20%	15%	$20,000	$21,500	$12,000	$12,810	5	Budget increase: Refer to Project Status report dated 02/21/09
2									
3									
4									
5									
6									

Comment: _____

Figure 13.2 A Sample Program Status Record.

- Providing a common standard for all of the different projects, allowing them to be subjected to equal and consistent comparison tools

Using past experience and industry standards, the PMO can derive the "right" metrics, which are capable of presenting snapshots of the project environment. The metrics are included in regular reports to the project committee. It is up to the project managers to take action on issues arising from the metrics evaluation.

Project performance metrics should include the following key elements:

- Budget metrics
- Schedule metrics
- Resource metrics

Budget Metrics

Budget performance metrics should be able to accomplish, but not be limited to, the following:

- Ensuring the appropriate expenditure is available for project completion
- Acting as an alert system to project authorities when expenditures are heading for a potential blowout
- Establishing expenditure authorization limit and escalation levels
- Establishing criteria for contingency funding

Schedule Metrics

Schedule performance metrics should be able to accomplish one major thing: establish whether the project is ahead of or behind schedule. The metrics will compare its planned schedule to actual progress.

Resource Metrics

Resource metrics should be able to accomplish, but not be limited to, the following:

- Measuring the number of human resources used in the different stages of the project

- Measuring the amount of project work that can be completed by a certain number of resources

- Indicating the number of resources needed to expedite a project

- Comparing the number of resources utilized versus expended budget and project completion rate

- Measuring resource availability versus resource requirements

Examples of the Use of Metrics

All these metrics should assist with corrective actions. In other words, the metrics are indicators when a project's progress is about to derail. The metrics should be generic enough so that they can be applied to various projects in the organization. The concept of having performance metrics is not something new and it has been explored in-depth by other disciplines, such as in process improvement (e.g., the Six Sigma© method). The following very basic examples present the concept to illustrate the use of metrics in a project environment.

Example 1

The following metric compares the amount of expenditure over the total budget and the amount of project completed.

Metric Indicators

- Total amount of budget that was approved to complete the project (X)

- Actual amount of budget that has been expended so far (Y)

- Estimated budget needed to complete the project (Z)

- Percentage of budget expended (*PBE*)

- Percentage of project completion (based on project schedule) (*PPC*)

These indicators are used to construct the budget progress ratio (BPR):

$$BPR = \frac{Y + Z}{X}$$

We can then set up the success level brackets to measure the project's performance:

- *BPR* > 1: If the forecasted expenditure turns out to be true, the project will be over the budget.

- *BPR* > 0.8. The project has high potential to exceed the budget.

- *BPR* < 0.5. The project is well under the budget.

Suppose that Project Laundromat has been allocated a $1 million budget and that it is to be completed within 10 months, from January 1, 2009, to October 31, 2009. On May 31, 2009, the project manager of Project Laundromat reports that $700,000 has been expended so far, and $200,000 is estimated to complete the project.

In this case,

$$BPR = \frac{\$700,000 + \$200,000}{\$1,000,000} = 0.9$$

This should alert the project manager that the project has potential to be overbudget soon.

Example 2

Another way to utilize budget metrics is to compare it with project completion. Using the same project as in example 1, assume that it is completed at a constant rate (thus, 10 percent of the project is completed in one month).

On May 31, 2009, five months since the project commencement, 50 percent of the project has been completed. Thus:

Percentage project completed (PPC) = 50%

$$PBE = \frac{\$700{,}000}{\$1{,}000{,}000} = 70\%$$

Because $PBE > PPC$, it can be said that the expenditure outspends the project completion. This too should alert the project manager on a possible budget blowout by the end of the project. If the discrepancy between the two metrics (PBE and PPC) are comparably large (the PMO should define the "success bracket", i.e., how much "large" is), then the project manager needs to take control measures to get the project back on track.

4. Program Status Reporting

Bearing in mind that the purpose of reporting is to convey an accurate picture of a project's status, based on the project's update and review, the following information should be captured by the PMO's reports to the project committee:

◻ Business cases and program plans submitted by project offices for approval by the project committee

◻ Project financials information, both the actual amount and planned budget

◻ Reconciliation of the project office's financial record with the finance department's record

- Summary of the completion status of all current projects (actual completion versus the planned schedule and the current phase or gate level)

- List of issues encountered in projects, whose solutions await the project committee's decisions

- Summary information for each project (projects' key players: project sponsors, project managers, project team members, and so on)

- The project's rank, which lists the projects according to how important they are to the organization (see Chapter 11)

- Summary of other relevant project information, such as the number of variations already approved for each project, the type of changes applied to the projects, and so on

5. Program Control

In monitoring the program, the PMO will always find projects that have gone too far off their schedules for many reasons (e.g., changes in project scope, a lack of resources, and so on). Most PMOs do not have the authority or the capabilities to exercise enough project control to bring these projects back on schedule. However, it can identify projects that are off track, identify the issues that need to be resolved, and escalate them (through the program report) to the program steering committee to make the decision. The program steering committee (which consists of business executives with the authority to make decisions) has the power to take measures, such as getting more resources—from either inside or outside the company—for the projects, extending the projects' deadline, increasing the projects' budget, and so on. Note also that since the whole process is iterative, the PMO will still have to monitor the projects' progress once the control is implemented and report back to the program steering committee.

An Escalation Model

A part of the program control is project issues *escalation*, a process where issues that cannot be resolved by the project manager will be presented to more senior executives (e.g., the project's sponsor, the project steering committee, or even the CEO), who will have the final say. Steps and processes followed in the escalation model can be similar to the dispute resolution model in the organization. The presence of a third independent party, such as the PMO, is necessary because it gives more credibility to the decision in the eyes of the disputing parties.

Making a Case for PMO: PMO and the Politics of Escalation

One aspect of escalation that doesn't get mentioned very often is office politics and how easy it is for the PMO to be trapped in the middle. And that's exactly what happened to Paul Witten, the PMO manager. He had been noticing how Jeremy Miller's project had been overbudget in the last three months. Paul was concerned about how the project's deficit seemed to snowball. Paul had discussed this with Jeremy, who kept assuring Paul that he could fix it himself. On one hand, Paul knew that unless he brought this issue to Dave's, the CEO's, attention, it would go unnoticed until it gets too big to handle. Paul also knew that it is the PMO's responsibility to escalate matters that, in the PMO's discretion, cannot be handled by the project manager. On the other hand, Jeremy's IT department was one of the PMO's biggest clients, and Jeremy was a good friend of Paul's. In the end, Paul decided to have one last talk with Jeremy, and he finally convinced him that it was better for his project if the budget issue was brought up to the CEO's attention for a better solution.

The first step involves the project manager's informing the PMO and requesting an issue resolution by a third party. In this instance, the PMO attempts to arbitrate the issues prior to escalating them to the next level. The PMO also documents the proceedings.

However, there are also instances when the escalation is initiated by the PMO, such as when the PMO identifies that a certain project is not run according to the organization's project management standard and is thus having negative impacts on the company (e.g., loss of money, project delay, and so on). In these circumstances, the PMO first discusses the matter with the particular project managers on their capabilities in correcting the problems, before escalating the issues to senior executives.

When an issue cannot be resolved at the project level, there are a number of escalation levels (refer to Figure 13.3), each taking the

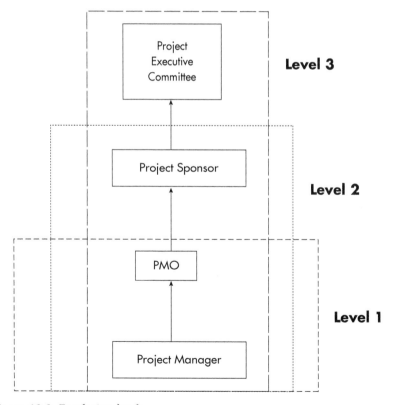

Figure 13.3 Escalation levels.

issue to the next higher level of management. At each level, the authority, in consultation with other stakeholders, will attempt to provide a timely resolution to the issues.

Level 1

The project manager escalates issues related to clients, vendors, or other third parties (for example, contract-related disputes over the terms of budget or completion date) to the PMO. Usually, the type of issues brought up to the PMO are more project related and small in scale (in comparison to issues brought up to Levels 2 and 3). The PMO then acts as an independent arbiter between the project and the other party (i.e., it reviews the contract and facilitates a negotiation between the two parties).

Level 2

When project issues cannot be resolved within the project, even with the assistance of the PMO, then the PMO facilitates the escalation process to the project sponsor. Thus, in the preceding example, assuming the PMO cannot resolve the contract dispute, it brings it up to the senior executive who's in charge of overseeing the project. For example, if the project is commissioned by the research and development department, the departmental head will have more authority than the PMO to make a decision to, say, allocate more money from the department to the project, thus ending the dispute with, say, the vendor.

Level 3

When issues still cannot be resolved by the project sponsor, the PMO escalates them to the project executive committee level. The committee, which has the company's senior executives (e.g., CEO, CFO, member of the board of directors, and so on), takes into account inputs from the project managers, the PMO, the clients and vendors, and the project sponsors to come up with a resolution. The project executive committee's decision is final.

Conclusion

The PMO's responsibility for managing the organization is the most complex role it has on its plate. It is an iterative process that involves various parties with varying interests, making it a delicate balancing act. In this chapter, we decided to not delve too much into the political issues (whose resolutions and negotiation methods have been provided in numerous managerial books). Instead, we equipped readers with simple tools that will allow the PMO to carry out its program monitoring and control tasks in the most objective manner.

5 Things You Need to Remember from This Chapter

1. The five stages in the iterative program monitoring and control process (information gathering, updating, reviewing, reporting, and controlling)

2. The items to be included in a program status report

3. The different metrics (for budget, resource, and schedule) to help the PMO in measuring a project's performance

4. The control measure that can be taken to bring projects back on track

5. The aim of issues escalation and the overall process as managed by the PMO

Project Audit

Projects rarely run according to their schedules or within their budgets. Most projects, in fact, run over speed bumps. This is when having proper project management standards becomes important because they provide guidance on how to prevent such situations from occurring and take proper course of action when they do. In the previous chapters, we have discussed the different ways in which the PMO can create such guidelines, from managing customers to reviewing the progress of a whole program. Now that we have all of these measures in place, the question is whether anyone will follow them.

The PMO has an inherent interest and responsibility to the organization in ensuring that all projects adhere to project management standards and guidelines, that all projects are run in the most efficient and effective manner, and that all projects hold up the organization's business values and ethics. To carry out this responsibility, the PMO needs to implement project audits. A *project audit* is a three-fold process.

◻ First, it allows the PMO to validate whether the project teams are utilizing the appropriate project management processes.

○ Second, the auditing process can be an opportunity for coaching the project managers to understand how the methodology is (or could have been) applicable to their project.

○ Third, it can provide feedback to the PMO when certain parts of the project standards or methodology are outdated or need improvement.

Project auditing is a stand-alone service that can also be outsourced to external consultants. In some cases, having an outside party perform the audits gives the process an added air of legitimacy that will prompt senior management to pay extra attention. However, a well-equipped PMO is more than capable to handle the task. As a kind of third party, the PMO is the most suitable entity within the organization to conduct the audit because it doesn't have overarching interest over either the project's client or the project's managers. In this chapter we will discuss what is involved in the PMO's role in auditing the projects and the methodology itself.

The PMO's Role in Project Audit

The auditing process can be carried out in the middle of a project, particularly when the monitoring process (discussed in Chapter 13) picks up strong alerts that the project is about to fail. However, the audit is more commonly carried out at the end of the project. Either way, the process needs the complete support of both project managers (who might have to disclose sensitive information) and senior management (who will actually implement the necessary changes upon receiving the audit results). As a part of its auditing role, the PMO is responsible for the following:

○ Ensuring that the projects comply with the organization's project management standards and other organizational policies

- Keeping all project-related guidelines and policies valid and up-to-date according to the industry's standard

- Ensuring that lessons learned are properly recorded as part of knowledge management so that past mistakes will not be repeated in future projects

- Ensuring that the audit process is unbiased, without any undue influence from other parties

It is very important that the end result presented by a project audit is a detailed, factual, and impartial analysis of how the project was managed. For derailed projects, the result can be a useful indicator to assist decision makers on whether to continue or stop the project. For failed projects, the audit results give directions on how to avoid similar mistakes in the future. For successful projects, the results highlight all the right things to do that should be adopted by future projects.

Project Audit Methodology

Bearing in mind that the project audit is a means to examine individual performance and the overall project performance, the PMO has to demonstrate a high degree of professionalism. This can be achieved by ensuring proper processes and procedures in conducting the audits. The audit process should include the following elements:

- Audit preparation
- Conducting the project audit
- Reporting the project audit
- Reviewing the audit result
- Follow-up actions

Audit Preparation

□ *Identify the audit team.* The formation of an audit team should include consideration of such matters as the required skills, where the team will be sourced from (whether the organization has sufficient skills or external experts are required), and how long the audit engagement will be.

□ *Determine the audit timing.* The timing of a project audit depends on the organization's need for oversight and assurance of the projects' progression. Such an audit may be conducted in the interim, with the frequency (monthly, bimonthly, and so on) to be determined based on various factors such as project scale, complexity, and priority. Interim audits are useful to spot project irregularities and perform corrections early on. Project audits can also be performed at the end of the project, at which time the emphasis is on the overall project performance and lessons learned.

□ *Determine audit tools.* Various wide-ranging audit tools can be used to achieve a comprehensive result, such as:

- Documents review (meeting minutes, risk and issue logs, progress reports, and so on)

- Interviews with project participants

- A checklist noting compulsory items to be accomplished

- Customer feedback and evaluation form

Conduct Project Audit

Prior to conducting a project audit, the PMO has to have a firm grip on how extensive the review needs to be and, based on that assessment, develop success criteria (e.g., the targeted performance level), like those shown in Figure 14.1, for every project. These criteria

Project Name: Project Sample

	Project Success Criteria		Project Variation	Rate
	Variation	**Rate**		
Budget: Compare actual budget versus planned budget. Higher negative variation (when actual > planned) results in higher rating.	>50%	3	40%	2
	30%–50%	2		
	0%–30%	1		
Schedule: Compare actual schedule versus planned schedule. Longer duration than planned results in higher rating.	**Variation**	**Rate**	70%	3
	>50%	3		
	30%–50%	2		
	0%–30%	1		
Resource: Compare actual number of resources versus planned resources. Negative variation (when there are more resources used than planned) results in higher rating.	**Variation**	**Rate**	20%	1
	>50%	3		
	30%–50%	2		
	0%–30%	1		

Note: Rating level indicates project performance, with highest rating indicating significant diversion from plan.

Figure 14.1 A sample project audit summary.

Making a Case for the PMO: The PMO and Project Audit

Two years ago, the PMO was a new business unit. It was still trying to figure things out, forging new relationships with clients, and shaping its own project standards. Back then, Paul Witten, the PMO manager, was in a meeting with his two senior project managers, Kerry Murphy and Bill Clements. The meeting topic was "How to determine a fair project metric for auditing purposes?" Paul had been mulling over the same question for over an hour now and asked, "Since each project has different characteristics, how do we know what would be the fair value to set a standard on?" Bill replied, "That's a good question. A ten percent budget deficit could be bad for one project but means nothing for another." After spending another two hours trying to determine one set of standardized values that can be applied in auditing all of the projects in the organization, they all finally agreed that such numbers that deem a project a success or a failure would be different for each project and that they should be set at the beginning of every project audit. "If we want to be fair, we need to look at this on a case-by-case basis. We should determine the failure or success criteria for every project separately after a discussion with the project manager and other parties in the project to fully understand what the project is about," said Paul, whose statement ended the meeting.

should reflect the ideal situation or benchmark for that particular project. They act as a reference point that the auditors can use to evaluate the actual project situation.

The following are some aspects of the project that must be considered in an audit:

- Business case
- Project plan
- Communications management
- Vendor and contractor management
- Project resource management
- Project cost management
- Project schedule management
- Customer satisfaction
- Risk management

A checklist that represents an overview of items for the PMO to consider during its audit exercise, like the one presented in Figure 14.2, is a useful audit tool.

Report Project Audit

Upon completion of a project audit, the findings from the process are compiled in a report. Information contained in the audit report should be tailored according to what is required by the project decision makers. However, the following fundamental aspects should always be included:

- Comparison between actual project performance and success criteria
- Identification of issues in the project execution
- Capturing lessons learned from both the successful and unsuccessful elements of the project

Review Audit Result

Upon receiving the audit report, the project committee should assess any issues or failures in more depth to get at the root of the cause. The project committee is also responsible for making decisions on future actions aimed at rectifying the project impacts, bringing the

(text continues on page 168)

Business Case	
Business case has been approved by all relevant authorities prior to progression to the next stage.	☐
Business case is aligned with the organization's strategy.	☐
Cost-Benefit Analysis was completed according to PMO's standard.	☐

Project Plan and Approach	
Risk response strategy has been developed in the planning stage.	☐
Project contingency plan has been developed in the planning stage.	☐
Project plan considers the appropriate industry standards and regulations.	☐
Project plan outlines the change management procedure.	☐
Project approach has been compared with industry benchmark.	☐

Risk Management	
Types of risks encountered in the project have been documented.	☐
Risks are reviewed at specified intervals.	☐
Risks' level of impacts and probability of occurring are documented.	☐
Mitigation actions and other details (person responsible for action, impacts of action on the project, etc.) have been documented.	☐

Project Cost Management	
Cost performance (actual versus planned) has been reviewed.	☐
Cost variance and its reason have been identified, recorded, and reviewed regularly.	☐
Expenditure is recorded and reported accurately according to PMO standard.	☐
Revenue is recorded and reported accurately according to PMO standard.	☐

Figure 14.2 A sample project audit checklist.

Project Schedule Management	
Schedule performance (actual versus planned) has been reviewed.	☐
Schedule variance and its reason has been identified, recorded, and reviewed regularly.	☐
Project progress is tracked accurately according to PMO standard.	☐
Project Resource Management	
Individual team member's performance review is conducted regularly in collaboration with the HR department.	☐
Resource level usage (actual versus planned) has been reviewed.	☐
Resource variance and its reason has been identified, recorded, and reviewed regularly.	☐
Resource selection process adheres to the PMO and HR guideline.	☐
Resource engagement and dispersion process is according to the PMO and HR guideline.	☐
Technology resources performance is documented and reviewed regularly.	☐
Customer Satisfaction	
Customers' feedback is sought and documented regularly.	☐
Contracts with customers specify deliverables, schedule, and resources required according to the PMO's guideline.	☐
Project deliverables have been signed off by the customers.	☐
Customer issues and responses (action taken, person responsible for action, and time taken to respond) are documented.	☐
Vendor and Contractor Management	
Contract administration activities adheres to the PMO's standard.	☐
Vendors' performance is recorded and reviewed regularly.	☐
Vendors' selection process adheres to the PMO's guideline.	☐
Vendors' deliverables are signed off by the relevant project authorities.	☐
Communications Management	
Progress report is regularly communicated to project stakeholders.	☐
Content of report adheres to the PMO guideline.	☐

project back on track, and improving the organization's project management capability. Any decisions made based on the audit result should be communicated to all relevant parties.

Follow-Up Actions

The last stage in the audit process involves the PMO's implementing the decisions made in collaboration with the project manager, project sponsor, and other project participants. For projects that are still running, the impacts of those actions will still be monitored by the PMO after a certain period of time. This postaudit stage may become an iterative process between senior management and project managers. For projects that have been terminated or closed, the outcome of such audits (e.g., a change in project management standard) could be referred to when completing future projects.

Conclusion

In this chapter, we have seen how a project audit is a vital piece in perfecting an organization's project management capability. The auditing process will not be an easy task for anyone to carry out. The full cooperation from project managers and senior managers is necessary. However, the task has to be done. By incorporating auditing process into its role, the PMO continuously pushes for improvement.

5 Things You Need to Remember from This Chapter

1. The purpose of conducting project audit
2. Why the PMO is the best party within the organization to conduct the process
3. The stages involved in a project audit
4. The use of audit tools such as a checklist and a project rating
5. The importance of cooperation from both project managers and senior management to conduct a successful audit

Systems to Drive the PMO

The success of the PMO is very much dependent on its ability to receive, process, and deliver information as simply as possible. Accordingly, the PMO needs an automated system that facilitates the mechanisms of communication, decision making, and control between the PMO and the project teams. With this in mind, we made the goal of this chapter to examine the characteristics of a suitable information system (i.e., software and its supporting systems) for the PMO and to describe the best way to obtain it. We will review the different areas that should be integrated into the same system, how the existing process may need to change to accommodate the new system, and how to determine whether the software and systems required should be purchased or developed in-house.

Introducing the New System

Current industry trends are moving toward off-the-shelf software packages that enable organizations to combine various project management functions (such as time entry, resource planning, cost estimates, and so on) with a view to determining project priority and ultimately whether the project has value. Although these packages offer many options and can deliver much of what is promised, the software often goes unused by those at whom it is aimed. The implementation of a new system often requires a seismic change in organizational culture (especially if it is being introduced for the first time) before it is accepted. If the processes surrounding the new system are not updated to be receptive of it, then you will be left with underutilized software and many disgruntled users (e.g., if users have to report time spent on projects in two different systems, one for payroll and one for the PMO, chances are they will end up out of sync). Bottom line: The PMO's automation will not deliver a return on investment!

To introduce a new system, the existing program management processes and practices should be redeveloped to incorporate and integrate all facets of the PMO's responsibility. The choice of system and software for the PMO must take the following aspects into consideration:

- Because the PMO must assist the senior management team in making decisions while providing supports to the project teams, the software must allow for a bottom-up flow of information (e.g., the system will capture information at project level and aggregate it at program level to be reviewed by management), as well as a top-down flow of decision making (e.g., the system will apply any changes to the program—budgetwise, schedulewise, personnelwise, and so on—at the program level first before dispersing them to individual projects).

- The same system, while supporting the project management process (e.g., project planning, time entry, cost distribution, and so on) must also provide executive information that reports on project health, portfolio health, and ultimately program health. The PMO will generally use the same toolsets used at project level and adapt them to capture and disperse information at program level, showing the required information for all projects and processes underway in the program that the PMO is monitoring. Figure 15.1 shows an example of a budgeting toolset and how the information moves up from its

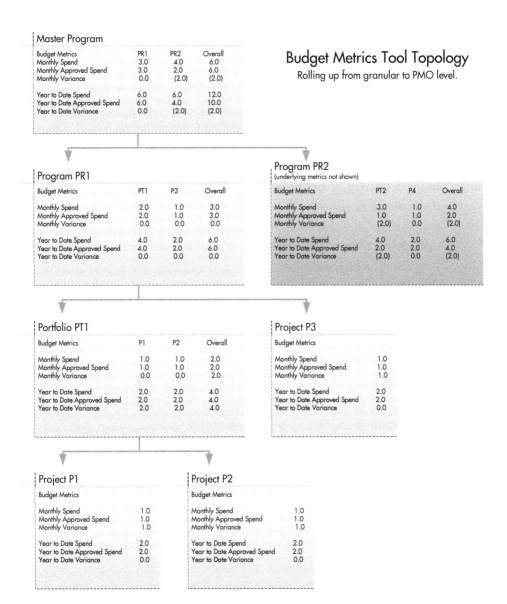

Figure 15.1 Topology for budget metrics: Rolling up from project to PMO.

most granular representation at project level all the way to the PMO. The same tool can also be used by the PMO to enforce best practices, review status, and determine program health budgetwise.

Integrating the Disparate Systems

In his book, *The Rise of the Project Workforce: Managing People and Projects in a Flat World* (2007), Rudolf Melik determines six key project practices that should be integrated to facilitate project workforce management: time and expense tracking, cost and revenue tracking, workforce planning, project planning, project process planning, and project analytics. What he describes are also the key areas of information to be managed by a PMO's system. Each item is applicable at both project and program levels.

The example shown in Figure 15.2, although simple, provides some context when considering which areas should be integrated for program management purposes. Each of the processes noted is a discipline in its own right, and in practice this translates to the different methods in capturing the data (i.e., various software, such as e-mail, word processing software, spreadsheets, enterprise resource planning [ERP] software, customer relationship management [CRM] software, time management software, project management software, cost management software, human resource management software, and so on, will be used). Thus, it is obvious that integrating data derived at project level is difficult. All of the systems have separate input requirements, run on different platforms, generate multiple result sets in different formats, and have separate security or access requirements that are difficult to centralize. Many of the systems are heavily customized, rendering them unsuitable for enterprisewide deployment.

Therefore, it is important to highlight that when introducing a centralized PMO system, the PMO's goal should be to combine the features of the systems that are used across the different areas into

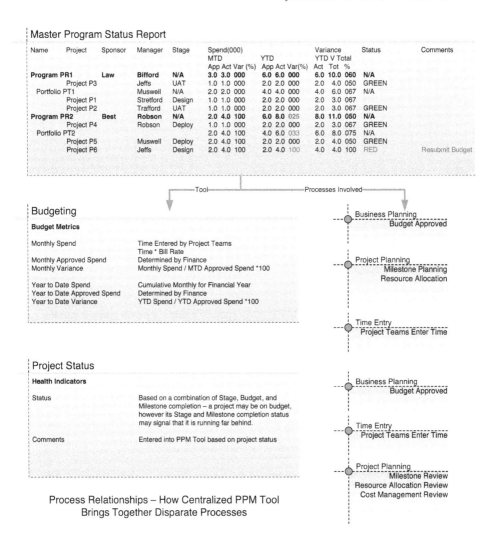

Master Program Status Report

Name	Project	Sponsor	Manager	Stage	Spend(000) MTD App Act Var (%)	YTD App Act Var(%)	Variance YTD V Total Act Tot %	Status	Comments
Program PR1		**Law**	**Bifford**	**N/A**	3.0 3.0 000	6.0 6.0 000	6.0 10.0 060	**N/A**	
	Project P3		Jeffs	UAT	1.0 1.0 000	2.0 2.0 000	2.0 4.0 050	GREEN	
Portfolio PT1			Muswell	N/A	2.0 2.0 000	4.0 4.0 000	4.0 6.0 067	N/A	
	Project P1		Stretford	Design	1.0 1.0 000	2.0 2.0 000	2.0 3.0 067		
	Project P2		Trafford	UAT	1.0 1.0 000	2.0 2.0 000	2.0 3.0 067	GREEN	
Program PR2		**Best**	**Robson**	**N/A**	2.0 4.0 100	6.0 8.0 025	8.0 11.0 050	**N/A**	
	Project P4		Robson	Deploy	1.0 1.0 000	2.0 2.0 000	2.0 3.0 067	GREEN	
Portfolio PT2					2.0 4.0 100	4.0 6.0 033	6.0 8.0 075	N/A	
	Project P5		Muswell	Deploy	2.0 4.0 100	2.0 2.0 000	2.0 4.0 050	GREEN	
	Project P6		Jeffs	Design	2.0 4.0 100	2.0 4.0 100	4.0 4.0 100	RED	Resubmit Budget

——————Tool———————————————Processes Involved——————

Budgeting

Budget Metrics

Monthly Spend	Time Entered by Project Teams Time * Bill Rate
Monthly Approved Spend	Determined by Finance
Monthly Variance	Monthly Spend / MTD Approved Spend *100
Year to Date Spend	Cumulative Monthly for Financial Year
Year to Date Approved Spend	Determined by Finance
Year to Date Variance	YTD Spend / YTD Approved Spend *100

Business Planning
Budget Approved

Project Planning
Milestone Planning
Resource Allocation

Time Entry
Project Teams Enter Time

Project Status

Health Indicators

Status	Based on a combination of Stage, Budget, and Milestone completion – a project may be on budget, however its Stage and Milestone completion status may signal that it is running far behind.
Comments	Entered into PPM Tool based on project status

Business Planning
Budget Approved

Time Entry
Project Teams Enter Time

Project Planning
Milestone Review
Resource Allocation Review
Cost Management Review

Process Relationships – How Centralized PPM Tool
Brings Together Disparate Processes

Figure 15.2 How the program tool can combine project processes.

a single package that will satisfy (as far as possible) all users. You need to consider several factors in the drive to create a solution that will fit your organization. Let us assume at this point that there is a reasonable budget in place and that we have resources available to do the work. (We will discuss how to get to that point later in the chapter.)

Getting the Desired System

Review the Systems in Use

First things first. Your project teams already use something to determine the health of their projects. Find out what it is and how they do it! If no standard is mandated, there will be major differences across your project management teams. You will see spreadsheets, project management software, paper (and a pen), or a combination of all three. For each area you would like to integrate (and automate, if necessary), determine the current process.

- Find out how stakeholders get their information and what they use it for.

- From the executive team, determine which reports they find the most useful and on what basis they use them to make decisions.

- Question the project management teams to understand how data is entered and what methods and reports they use to ascertain project health.

- Determine from all stakeholders what they see as their priority items, the must-haves if everything is integrated.

- Note the data storage methods for each of the systems, and decide how data extraction will be facilitated. This is a key factor of integration and should be reviewed for each channel.

Once a study of those systems in place has been executed, review the packages available to determine whether one of them will support your objectives. Here are some factors to consider:

- *Budget.* This is the primary decision factor, and it narrows your range of choices considerably.

- *Timing.* When do you need the processes to be up and running?

- *Software.* Look at the service offering for each channel you have chosen to automate. Maybe a package is very strong in one area but weak in another (e.g., strong budget and fore-casting but weak resource management or project reporting).

▫ *Organization.* How mature is the vendor company? Can you depend on them to be around next year? Because you are choosing software that will support your decision-making process for a lengthy period of time, your vendor should be able to do the same.

▫ *Data Storage, Extraction, and Manipulation.* Can you import data easily from the existing systems?

▫ *Reporting.* Most project management processes live and die by the reports they produce. Will the packages under investigation be able to generate suitable reports?

▫ *Horsepower.* Do you have the equipment to run the software, and, if not, does your budget cover the upgrade?

Build Versus Buy

The next thing to consider is how to get the system. Should we buy it or build it?

First, let us define "build" and "buy." *Build* means that your organization will create the software to support the PMO and that you will get what you want (in theory). *Buy*, on the other hand, will see you either purchase or license existing software from an application service provider (ASP) that may be close to your needs but does not fit exactly and outsource the integration of that software into your existing systems.

Many off-the-shelf applications can assist the PMO in the quest for system integration into a single workflow. They vary in price from hundreds to millions of dollars, depending on the need. Much progress has been made in the development of program management software because the processes themselves have become better defined (thanks to standards introduced by organizations such as PMI). Many vendors have vanilla offerings that are easily customizable to fit the needs of the PMO. At the time of writing, companies such as Primavera, Microsoft, Compuware, IBM, HP PPM, SAP, Borland, Oracle, and Planview all deliver fully integrated product suites that enable program management. The key driver behind the growth of this industry is the need for companies of all sizes to gain a better understanding of how their product investment contributes to the bottom line.

Vendor software may suit some installations, but for others there may be good reasons to buy. Some companies may want to integrate their existing proprietary applications into a PMO program system. Complexities and nuances of these systems may render customization out of the question. Involvement of a third party may also result in the exposure of sensitive information. Indeed, the organization's culture may drive the choice of buy versus build (generally, pioneering organizations choose to build, and more conservative companies opt to learn from the mistakes of others*). So how can the PMO determine which approach is better suited to achieve its aims?

There are many considerations to examine when deciding whether to build or buy: time to market, whether the introduction of the software is to gain competitive advantage, cost, existing infrastructure, corporate culture, expertise availability, and so on.

Here is a list of reasons for choosing to build software instead of buying it:

The Build Advantage

- Protection of proprietary systems and information against outsiders

- Only internal stakeholders involved

- Outside vendors not required

- Ability to address system requirements accurately

- No need to customize the platform to meet requirements

- Usually lower operation cost, with a greater percentage of the cost absorbed during the development of the product, requiring a higher investment at start of project

---

*Neil Chandler, "Analytic Applications: Buy vs. Build vs. Customize," Gartner Research, November 2, 2007.

- Lower licensing and maintenance costs than for purchased software

- Easier change control because it is not governed by outside requirements.

- Easier integration into existing corporate systems.

Here is a list of reasons for choosing to buy software instead of building it:

The Buy Advantage

- Reduced risk of not delivering the product on time

- Freed-up resources, enabling the technical teams to work on other projects (i.e., less opportunity cost)

- Usually a favorable lead time, getting the process up and running quicker than a build endeavor

- Sometimes cheaper than building

The opportunities afforded by each approach are accompanied by some kind of risk.

Build and Buy Disadvantages

- The *build* option is constrained by time, budget, and resources. If the introduction of the system is to help the organization gain competitive advantage, the time to market the build option may be a hindrance. Deciding to build exposes the enterprise to the risk of delay or failure.

- Alternatively, *purchasing* may result in changes to existing procedures not related to the integration effort (e.g., a change to payroll systems initiated by changes in time reporting). The ongoing costs associated with a buy may be higher than the build option depending on how much customization is required.

Table 15.1 summarizes the different areas to consider in deciding whether to buy or build the system.

Table 15.1 Build Versus Buy: What to Consider

Areas of Consideration	Build	Buy
Team skill sets	Build if requirements are determined to be within the skill set of the existing development teams.	Products may be available to execute the process, though none is an exact fit.
Proprietary systems	Linkage to proprietary company systems outside the PMO realm may be more straightforward because project teams will have knowledge of them.	Implementation may be cost-effective, but customization might be expensive. The vendor will generally not be familiar with the systems that are to be integrated.
Data Integration	If data integration is required from internal systems under development, the data may change.	Expenses include ongoing maintenance and licensing.
Resource availability	The company has the sources available to develop application.	Time to market is generally quicker when customization is minimal.
Opportunity cost	Opportunities may be lost due to the time required by project teams to build software that could be spent working on other endeavors.	Opportunities may be explored because development time is minimized.
Development cost	Initial development cost is generally higher, but ongoing maintenance should be lower.	The purchase cost will be lower, but ongoing maintenance and licensing charges will be more expensive.
Time to market	Systems developed in-house are generally slower due to resource availability, project management processes, etc.	Most vendors will have a preliminary package that can be in place fairly quickly. However, customization may slow the process down somewhat.
Risk	Risk is taken on by organization.	Bulk of risk taken on by a third party.
Customization	At the outset, an existing vanilla package poses no constraints; however, as other organization systems mature or change, major changes may be required.	Software is expensive to customize. Vendors realize much income from system customization.
Privacy	Company processes and procedures are kept in-house.	Sensitive information may be exposed to outside persons.

The Case for the PMO: Software Build Versus Buy

Now that FAS Inc.'s PMO had started to change the processes by which projects were managed, they were charged by the management team with introducing a new system that could integrate their timekeeping, resource allocation, budgeting, and project planning tools. Up to this point, each project manager had executed his or her own set of spreadsheet formulas, which seemed to give different results depending on who was managing the project.

The PMO decided to evaluate the company's ability to build the software. The systems team were extremely flexible and deliver very high-quality work, but challenges arising from other projects would require reprioritization if they were to develop the new software. The team decided to complete a build versus buy exercise to determine the viability of building the application themselves. Their primary objective was to determine the opportunity cost versus the development cost. Time saved not developing the software could be put to good use with resulting products, generating revenues that would offset the difference in purchase cost in the long run. The build-versus-buy matrix that follows shows how they arrived at the decision to purchase the software.

Build-Versus-Buy Matrix, FAS Inc. Service Center Software
Recommendation: Purchase—Although we have the in-house expertise to create the software, expert packages are available that we believe could be introduced in a relatively short time. The major risk that we see for building is the ensuing delay to the new FAS Prime software release, which will lead to an opportunity cost of over $75,000. Although there is a difference in price of some 16 percent for purchasing the software, we believe that the extra cost will be recouped over the life of the application.

Areas of Consideration	Build	Buy
Team skill sets	The team is not really familiar with the engine that would drive such a process, but they do have the skills that could be used to develop once training is undertaken.	HP and IBM product suites both fit the needs of FAS Inc., although both would require consulting effort to install. Neither is quite an exact fit.
Proprietary systems	We can link into our current timekeeping and payroll systems, which would cut down on development time.	Vendors assure us that they could integrate any standard feed into the system with limited changes. This would require consulting and some work from our teams.
Data Integration	New feeds under development may change; we can update our system.	Changes to feed specifications will result in further work.
Resource availability	We have 5 resources that, with training, we would be able to get started within the next 2 months. We anticipate that they would be working on the project for 1 year.	System is ready to go.
Opportunity cost	It is estimated that the proprietary system will take 1 year to complete. We have 3 projects that would have to be postponed to accommodate that delivery schedule. • Revenue from proposed products over 2 years: $250,000 ($75,000 year 1; $175,000 year 2) • Cost to develop and deploy software: $100,500 • Delivery time: 1 year • Opportunity cost to develop in-house assuming no delays: $75,000	The opportunities cost decreases; in-house development time is minimized, although the actual cost is increased due to purchasing and customization costs. • Revenue from proposed products over 2 years: $250,000 ($75,000 year 1; $175,000 year 2) • Cost of software, including licensing: $120,500 ($12,000 in-house spending on development to support implementation) • Delivery time: 4 months. • Opportunity cost: $0 because there are no delays to development.
Development cost	Cost at $180,000 is lower; opportunity cost should be considered. • Development: $100,500 • Maintenance: $ 20,000 • Year 1: $100,500 • Subsequent: $20,000 • 5-year cost: $180,500	Overall, this looks more attractive when taking into account opportunity cost: • Purchase: $75,000 • License and support: $23,500 • One-off in-house: $12,000 • One-off customization: $10,000 • Year 1: $120,500 • Subsequent: $22,500 • 5-year cost: $210,500
Time to market	We expect delivery in roughly 1 year, but we could reduce this by using agile development to move the project forward. Best case is probably 8 months.	Ready to go in 4 months; however, we may need more customization. Would a fixed price solution be available?
Risk	Opportunity missed: The costs reviewed are only for year 1. Continual upgrades by our teams will result in unanticipated opportunity costs during the life of the application. Cost overruns are our responsibility	Unchecked customization costs eat into opportunity advantages.

Selecting the engine to drive the PMO is a major undertaking—indeed a project in its own right. Stakeholder and sponsor support is a key factor in the success of the delivery. The system should be flexible enough to encompass change when required but stable enough to be adopted and accepted as the PMO system for the organization. In other words, the system should be the solution that drives the organization by providing an invaluable insight into the value of each project.

Conclusion

In Part III of this book, we have discussed the various roles of the PMO. Each chapter outlines the tasks to be carried out by the PMO, as well as how those important responsibilities can positively affect an organization. Now that we have a firm understanding of what exactly a PMO does, in the next section we will discuss the steps taken to establish a PMO.

5 Things You Need to Remember from This Chapter

1. The main aim of having an automated system to support the PMO

2. The different areas in the organization from which data will be derived

3. The challenges in integrating project-level data into program data

4. The need to review the existing systems before introducing the new system that goes with the PMO

5. The different advantages and disadvantages of building or buying the system

PART IV

A BUSINESS DIVISION

Establishing a PMO

The greater challenge for any organization contemplating a PMO is ensuring that true value can be delivered to the organization. Such value can come in the form of greater efficiency and operation effectiveness, which translate to improved bottom line. Throughout the book, we have been highlighting the purpose of a PMO, which, in essence, is to help a company develop and sustain a competitive advantage by providing the right decision-making mechanisms, structure, processes, and control. All of these add value. At the beginning of the book, we emphasized the importance of justifying having a PMO in the organization as a wise business decision. We then looked at the multiple roles that the PMO plays, pointing out how it adds value to the organization along the way.

At this point, we hopefully have convinced you that adding a PMO can improve your organization's competitive advantage. You have created a business plan for the PMO, and the decision to establish a PMO has been justified (see Chapters 2 and 3) by senior management. If that's the case, we will now go one step further and look at the various ingredients needed to establish the PMO.

The PMO's Key Governing Entities

The first element to consider in establishing a PMO is the key governing entities (discussed later in the chapter). For the PMO to have sufficient authority to influence project management practice in the organization, an executive project committee must be established to facilitate its introduction and implementation (i.e., senior executives can sit on this board to oversee the establishment and the operation of the PMO). However, the support from nonexecutive participants (e.g., project managers, the end users, and others) is not any less important because they will be involved with the PMO's daily operation. The following is a list of key governing entities with an explanation of who they are and their importance to the success of the PMO. See Figure 16.1.

▫ *Executive Project Committee.* The project committee consists of executives who have vested interests in the PMO and who will act as the sponsors. The committee is responsible for all the ultimate decisions made on the project environment. The decisions it makes are wide-ranging, from approving project changes to arbitrating project disputes.

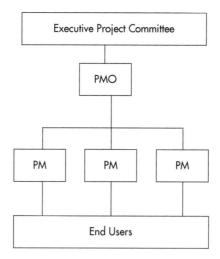

Figure 16.1 PMO governance entities.

- *Project Manager (PM).* Project managers act as the conduits for the PMO to improve the organization's project management capabilities. They implement project policies and guidelines under the PMO's instruction, and they deal directly with the end users of the PMO's project management services.

- *End Users.* The PMO must have a good rapport with the clients. To achieve that rapport, they first need to determine who specifically will be the potential clients, what their requirements will be, and how to best liaise with them. End users can be the various departments within the organization, vendors, and the organization's external customers.

The PMO Charter

The second element to consider is the PMO Charter. The purpose of the charter is to define the operational parameters of the PMO: its purpose, the services it offers, its sponsors, its customers, and so on. There are three fundamental keys to address in the PMO Charter:

1. The activities that will be undertaken in *establishing* the PMO
2. The activities that will be undertaken in *implementing* the PMO
3. The ongoing *operational* role of the PMO

First and foremost, the charter should capture the purpose of the PMO: the PMO is created to monitor, control, support, and continuously improve the organization's project management capability. The charter will be a living document that will be continuously adapted to the organization's strategic changes. Approved by the relevant authority, the PMO charter will serve the following mission:

- Define the PMO's purpose and alignment with the organization's business objectives (e.g., increase revenue, improve customer satisfaction, and so on)

- Detail the PMO's authority to accomplish its mission (the authority will mainly be on the development, implementation, and management of project management practices within the company). Such authority also includes examining how every project is carried out and taking corrective actions when project management practice diverges from the standards.

Note that, although official authority is sought for the PMO, there may be some reservations about how much direct control the PMO should have on each independent project, since other departmental heads could get defensive "protecting" their projects if they see the PMO as a threat. This potential conflict can be eliminated by having a clearly defined PMO charter. The following lists a number of items that must be included in a PMO charter:

- Identify the PMO's source of funding to acknowledge that the PMO is a valid operating unit, with business cost and revenue.

- Outline the PMO's main responsibilities, services, and functions.

- Define the PMO's structure and the responsibilities of key personnel.

- Determine where the PMO will fit into the organization's structure—a critical issue for the organization as a whole (what kind of structure it will have and who it will report to must clearly be addressed in the charter).

- Define the PMO's key performance indicators (KPIs), targets, milestones, and so on to measure its success (both internal and external benchmarks can be applied to measure PMO's performance over time).

- List the key governing entities within the organization.

A sample of a PMO Charter is in Appendix C.

Making a Case for PMO: Creating the PMO Charter

After all of the planning, Paul Witten was now ready to get his hands dirty and build a PMO from scratch. He knew that the charter would be the foundation the PMO needs, and it probably is the most important thing he needed to set up his PMO. He knew what to do.

The first thing he did was to set up meetings with the PMO's potential key governing entities: the executive committee (the CEO, the CFO, and the COO), senior project managers, and the end users (i.e., general managers) from the various departments. These meetings were more like brainstorming sessions. He really would like to know what everyone thinks the role of the PMO should be and how much they would support it. At every meeting, he kept a record of people's inputs. He then went back to them afterward to clarify any issues he felt was not adequately covered during the session. He also noticed that there were plenty of disagreements throughout the meetings on what people think the PMO's role should be. To solve this issue, he went to the executive committee to gain direction on what to do (he knew that he won't be able to make everyone happy anyway). Once he was sure that he fully understood what the whole organization (not the individual or the department) needs, he drafted the PMO charter and obtained the executive committee's approval. Once their approval was announced, it was so much easier for the PMO charter to gain acceptance.

Determining PMO Staffing

The PMO manager, in consultation with project managers and the PMO sponsors, decide on all the necessary staff and equipment to ensure that the PMO is able to do all the work defined in the charter. The PMO manager also needs to collaborate with the human resources department to recruit the right personnel. (Staffing the PMO is discussed in more detail in Chapter 19.)

Gathering the Required Facilities and Equipment

The availability of facilities and equipment is another prerequisite for successfully running the PMO. Their acquisition can be done in the following simple steps:

- *Step 1: Identify the facilities and equipment required.* An extensive exercise is needed to produce a comprehensive list of the facilities and equipment. The following items must definitely be on the list:

  - Work space that is large enough to accommodate all PMO personnel and that fulfills the Occupational Health and Safety (OSHA) standard

  - Office equipment such as telephone, computer, software, work desk, and the like

- *Step 2: Acquire the equipment and facilities.* The PMO should liaise with the appropriate department and personnel responsible for the company's asset management (usually the organization's administrative or facilities manager) to arrange assets acquisition within a specific time frame and budget.

- *Step 3: Manage assets.* The PMO is responsible for maintaining the company assets it's using. A record of all of the items acquired, upgraded, and disposed of is required, and it should contain information on the items' values, acquisition and disposal cost, and so on. The information will be required by the administrative department responsible for the overall assets management.

The checklist in Figure 16.2 represents a set of activities that must be carried out and items that must be acquired or developed for establishing the PMO.

Conclusion

The process of establishing a PMO can be a long and arduous one. In this chapter, we tried to cover all the aspects the PMO needs to consider, from gaining stakeholders' support to gathering the office equipment. Now that we have everything we need in place, in the next chapter we will discuss how to start integrating the PMO into the organization.

5 Things You Need to Remember from This Chapter

1. The key governance entities and the importance of gaining support from them

2. The purpose of a PMO charter (i.e., to define the parameter of the PMO's service)

3. The content of the PMO charter (e.g., PMO's objective, funding source, roles and authority, and so on)

4. The type of equipment needed to run the PMO and how to obtain it

5. The need for proper staffing has to be realized early on before implementing the PMO

PMO strategic plan	☐
PMO operational plan	☐
Outline of the PMO scope of responsibilities and authorities	☐
PMO budget (amount and source)	☐
PMO human resource management (skills, organizational structure, roles and responsibilities, training, salaries, and so on)	☐
Outline of the PMO processes (standardization through consultation, process improvements, creating templates, and so on)	☐
Program repository	☐
PMO charter	☐
PMO facilities (fax machine, telephone, and so on)	☐
PMO risks management plan (e.g., risk logs)	☐
PMO issues management plan (escalation procedure, and so on)	☐
PMO change management plan	☐
PMO communications management plan	☐
PMO knowledge management plan (knowledge repository, and so on)	☐
PMO reporting mechanisms	☐
PMO audit mechanisms	☐
PMO implementation plan (culture development, integration strategy, and so on)	☐
PMO organizationwide training programs	☐
PMO business liaison plan	☐

Figure 16.2 Checklist for establishing a PMO.

Implementing a PMO

The biggest challenge in implementing the PMO is dealing with organizational change. Just like any kind of change, the process will be faced with resistance. We will start this chapter with a discussion of change management, followed by a practical step-by-step method of integrating the PMO into the organization. Finally, we will also describe ways to set up the process to monitor the PMO's performance once it's established.

Implementing a Lasting Transformation

This discussion on change management is meant to provide guidance; it is intended to lead to specific and practical steps in implementing the PMO. Though throughout the chapter we will refer to a well-known author, whose ideas in change management have been widely adopted across various industries, we will not attempt to discuss change management in depth or to replicate the many texts already written on change management.

The general consensus is that change in an organization is a difficult process: It does not proceed in a linear fashion, it is influenced by many elements, it impacts many areas of the company, and it forces new patterns of interaction within the organization. This creates a high level of discomfort among employees. To handle this reaction, active leadership is required: Change implementation cannot be managed by only a few top managers. In fact, the whole process should include inputs from staffs of all levels. The better the employees understand the change, the better the chances are to gain their cooperation.

Dealing with Change in Integrating the PMO

The introduction of a PMO may be accompanied by a multiyear implementation plan that could disrupt "the way things are" and leave people feeling insecure, undervalued, or, worse, unneeded. Naturally, people's reaction is to resist change. Because, by far, this reaction is the biggest obstacle in implementing the PMO, we will first deal with this issue (i.e., where the resistance comes from, the type of resistance the PMO and its champion have to deal with, and how to handle those obstacles) before discussing the steps in PMO implementation.

In his book, *Project Management: A Systems Approach to Planning, Scheduling and Controlling* (2003), Harold Kerzner narrows down resistance to organizational change to two main areas: professional and personal.

◘ *Professional resistance* arises when the business units fear that change will affect them adversely. For example, the PMO may require the finance department to adopt new measures to approve project financing, or the technology unit may be required to use new time management software to manage various projects' resource allocation instead of using a spreadsheet. In both cases, the implementation of the PMO may create some resistance because it results in the adoption of new systems that will require a change in processes that people are already used to, which may lead to the perception that employees' workload will increase as the result.

- *Personal resistance* is generally caused by the fear that change will have negative impacts on the individuals: "How will the new structure change affect my career?" "Will I waste too much time trying to learn new processes under the PMO?"

Faced with resistance from both the institutional and individual level, what can the PMO leadership do to alleviate this? The following section provides the answer to the question.

Addressing Resistance at the Professional Level

To address resistance at the professional level, the first thing to do is to obtain the commitment of senior management. With them behind you, much of the professional resistance from various departments will dissipate. This commitment can be demonstrated in many ways: PMO empowerment (i.e., assigning authority to the office), financial support, visibility, and communication of the vision by the executive team are key components for success.

Ensure that the mandate for change is linked to the company's goals and success. It is difficult to oppose something that will benefit the organization. When met with resistance, address it and connect the answer to corporate vision: "We understand your concern about the increased workload, but the workload is temporary and, when your team completes the training, the newly acquired expertise will assist us in becoming a market leader in this field, which is one of the company goals for next year."

Look for opportunities to influence your audience. Whether on the corporate website, in the company newsletter, via e-mail, or at project meetings, always try to get your message out to those affected. Different approaches should be used for different facets of your audience; communicate the executive's commitment to the PMO to the rest of the organization, describe the expected benefits that will result from a successful PMO introduction, and so on.

Addressing Resistance at the Personal Level

To address resistance at the individual level, let us look at Kerzner's theory that personal resistance to change comes from four primary factors: change in work habits, change in social groups, embedded fears, and change in remuneration. He also focuses on five strategies to address these fears:

1. Explain the reasons for the change and get feedback.

2. Explain the desired outcomes and reasoning behind them.

3. Champion the change process.

4. Empower the change leaders.

5. Invest in training to support the changes once made.

Table 17.1 summarizes the types of resistance that may be experienced by the PMO and suggests some strategies to overcome them.

Introducing a new approach to an organization requires buy-in from all stakeholders to ensure a successful execution of the change plan. The following example, which is based on a real-life situation at FAS Inc., provides a snapshot of how the challenges may occur in the process of integrating the PMO into the organization.

If this scenario has occurred in your organization, you will understand that Paul had his work cut out for him at the beginning. However, he preempted those challenges by having a proper plan and by gathering support from senior management. That made his life much easier, and the PMO was successfully integrated into the organization.

Now that we have discussed the big picture of change management, we will conclude this chapter with concise step-by-step guidance on how to implement the PMO.

Table 17.1 Managing the Organization's Resistance to Change

Fear	Manifestation	Strategy to Overcome
Resistance: Social		
New relationships	Unwillingness to join new project teams	• Networking and team-building exercises
Multiple bosses	"Whom do I go to with a problem?"	• Acceptable pace of change • Properly empowered PMO and project managers • Laying out who is responsible for what
Multiple temporary assignments	"I'm overwhelmed."	• Maintaining functional management structure • Maintaining functional teams so participants have a home
Severing of established ties	"I don't know anyone I work with."	
Resistance: Work Habits		
New process and guidelines	Unwillingness to adopt	• Mandating conformity
Sharing of power information	Perceived loss of authority	• Identifying tangible and intangible benefits • Demonstrating executive management team support
Creation of fragmented work environment	"I don't know anyone who I work with."	• Maintaining functional teams so participants have a home
Need to give up established work patterns and learn new skills	"I used to be able to do my job, but now. . . ."	• Networking and team-building exercises with functional team
Resistance: Embedded Fears		
Failure	"What happens when I fail?"	• Educating workforce on benefits of change
Termination	"Will I lose my job?"	• Showing willingness to accept mistakes
Workload	"My job is difficult enough as it is."	• Showing willingness to pitch in
Unknown	"We don't know if this is going to help."	• Transforming unknowns into opportunities
Embarrassment	"I don't know how to use a computer."	• Sharing information
Fragmented organization	"How will my working relationship with staff from another department affected?"	
Resistance: Remuneration		
Shift of authority and power	"The PMO will absorb or reduce my authority to make decisions."	• Linking incentives to change
Lack of recognition	The PMO will get the kudos for project success	• Creating career path based on PMO processes
Unknown rewards and punishment	"Now that I report to multiple bosses, I don't know if I will be rewarded or castigated."	• Keeping functional management structure in place
Improper evaluation of personal performance	"Now that the organization is more projectized, how is my performance evaluated?"	
Multiple bosses		

Source: Adapted from Kerzner (2003).

A Case for PMO: Challenges in Implementing the PMO

Two years ago, when he started, Dave told Paul that his PMO would have complete control over program management, including authority over budget, staffing, and quality standards. He would be able to adjust team structure to give his project managers more authority.

Once handed his charter, Paul knew that he would have to get buy-in from everyone in the organization to make the efforts to introduce and maintain the PMO a success. To do this, he developed a comprehensive communication strategy and a resistance mitigation plan. He met with various stakeholders and presented the charter and his plan to implement it. He then solicited feedback to get a feel for the attitude from the general population. Once he knew the challenges he faced, he categorized them based on the professional and personal resistance types. He reviewed the teams and reached out to those who were recognized centers of influence and asked them to assist in getting acceptance from staff members. Once he had his influencers on board, Paul addressed the concerns individually, tying them to the company's mission and the mission of the PMO. He then presented these to his team and sent them on their way to evangelize the new changes with the resistance mitigation plan at hand to help. At the same time he had the executive sponsor, Dave, call a company meeting to launch the PMO, empower it, and lay out the upcoming changes and the timeframes. Then Paul went to each department and reviewed the plan again with the functional units that would be affected.

Steps in Integrating the PMO into the Organization

Integrating the PMO in a planned and sequential manner is vital in ensuring its success. The essence of change management just discussed can be captured in the following steps:

- *Step 1: Define and communicate the purpose of the PMO integration.* Before conducting any changes, the stakeholders who will be affected must be informed of the reasons for the change. They will ask for explanation as to why the change must take place, rather than blindly following orders. This is the opportunity for the PMO's supporters to explain the benefits of the PMO to the organization. Be specific about the expected outcomes, what exactly will be changed, how the change will be implemented, how that will affect the stakeholders, why the PMO is necessary, and, equally important, the consequences of not adopting the PMO.

  It is important to start talking about the changes early on, before the actual change takes place. A two-way formal consultative framework should be established, and informal communication must be encouraged. It should be clear to the rest of the organization that the implementation of the PMO is a collective effort and that all should be involved in the key discussions.

- *Step 2: Prepare a change management plan.* Just like a project plan, the change management plan allows you to scope the change processes. The plan should include the goals, milestones, timeframe, resources required, tasks (e.g., obtaining staff's commitment, conducting stakeholders information session, and so on), and who will be responsible for them. It is very important that the PMO's sponsors agree to and sign off on the plan because their support will be vital. The sponsors will also play an important role as an arbiter if problems are encountered during the implementation process. Good planning in the beginning can save you a lot of time and trouble as the transformation progresses.

◘ *Step 3: Conduct a stakeholders analysis.* Stakeholders can be thought of as groups of individuals who have a vested interest in the organization's ability to perform and to maintain viability in the short and long run. The primary objective of a stakeholder analysis is to identify the key individuals or groups who will be affected the most by the integration of the PMO, how their resistance can hold up the implementation process, and how their support can catapult the progress forward. Stakeholders can be employees, customers, suppliers, competitors, or other groups. The analysis should also determine the appropriate level of interaction with these stakeholders (i.e., whether they need to be informed or consulted on a specific action, whether their approval is required, etc.).

◘ *Step 4: Manage the human aspect of change management.* All types of organizational change will almost always elicit some emotional responses. This is the biggest part of managing the transformation. As mentioned, there are plenty of studies on psychological responses to change. Understanding these models will invariably help with the PMO integration process.

◘ *Step 5: Establish consultation and communication processes.* One of the most important rules in change management is that those affected should be given the opportunity to be involved in the change process. By adopting this principle, the PMO sponsors will entice people to be more positive toward the changes. A number of tools can be used as communication channels: e-mails, forums (both physical and electronic), surveys, interviews, among others.

◘ *Step 6: Develop evaluation strategies.* Evaluation strategies need to be built into the PMO integration plan to measure the level of success at every stage. The evaluation step should include (but not be limited to) a monitoring process (e.g., progress reports to the change leaders), a feedback review process (e.g., a proper channel for stakeholders to voice their opinions, either through e-mail or meetings), and performance indicators (e.g., timeliness of the progress, positive response from stakeholders, and so on).

Through effective change management, the integration of the PMO into the company can be carried out seamlessly. A sample integration plan for a PMO is provided in Appendix D.

Monitoring PMO Performance

If the PMO will operate as an independent business unit, then it is only fair that it is treated like any other unit in the organization, and that goes for monitoring its performance. The PMO's performance can be effectively monitored by comparing its actual performance against its corporate strategy, and to do that here are a couple of available tools:

◘ *Regular Status Report.* Just like any other business unit within the organization, the PMO should submit a regular status report for review by the executive committee. The report should include, among other things, the PMO's achievements since the last report, the PMO's forward actions, revenue and expenditure, and other relevant information based on the PMO's key performance indicators (KPI, explained in more detail in the next section). The format of the status report should follow the standard format applicable to the other business units in the organization. This will facilitate a fair comparison between the PMO and other business units' performance.

- *Audit Process.* An audit of the PMO's performance should be carried out by an independent party, either by the auditor from within the organization or by an external consultant. The audit will review the PMO's operation, processes, and procedures, as well as staff performance, against the organization's standards and guidelines. In addition to reviewing how the PMO conducts its business, the auditor should also review the PMO's overall performance, as reflected in its key performance indicators.

Key Performance Indicators

Having an effective performance management system in place calls for a good balance between the financial and strategic measures, addressing both short- and long-run objectives. R. Kaplan and D. Norton, in their book *The Strategy-Focused Organization* (2001), proposed that, when setting up key performance indicators, four major dimensions of organizational activity should be considered: financial, external, internal business process, and learning and growth. Using those four factors as reference, readers can set up their own PMO's KPI, for example:

- *Client.* These KPIs are aimed at measuring the quality of services provided by the PMO according to customers' perception. Client-focused KPIs may include, for example, client satisfaction level, client retention rate, PMO's knowledge on each client, and so on.

- *Effectiveness.* These KPIs are aimed at measuring the effectiveness of the PMO as a leader in the organization's project management environment. The KPIs measure areas such as the time it takes to develop and implement a new standard, acceptance level of new standards and guidelines, the time it takes for the PMO to respond to new project management regulations, the PMO's ability to customize service, its contribution to projects' success rate, the return on investment (ROI) on the PMO, and so on.

◘ *Expenditure.* Although the PMO's main aim is to provide services that support the organization's project management capability, not profit making, it is still important to measure cost performance. Examples of cost-focused KPIs include the PMO's running cost compared to the number of projects it monitors, the percentage of expenditure used to invest in assets (e.g., project management software) compared to the total expenditure, the amount of expenditure against the available budget, and so on.

Conclusion

In this chapter we highlighted the fact that the biggest obstacle in integrating the PMO into the organization comes from the people themselves. Human emotional reaction to change is the first thing to manage in the transformation process. Once this obstacle is overcome, the PMO can apply the more mechanical step-by-step method of implementing the change. We drew attention to the importance of having a change management plan to make sure that the process can flow smoothly. Once established, the PMO has to be monitored. We presented a couple of tools that can be used to measure its performance.

Now that we have the PMO established and operating, it needs a leader who can take it to reach its goals. This will be the topic of discussion for the next chapter.

5 Things You Need to Remember from This Chapter

1. The steps involved in transforming an organization

2. Where organizational resistance (personal and professional) will come from when the PMO is introduced

3. How to handle the resistance

4. The importance of having a plan to deal with change-related challenges before integrating the PMO

5. The tools that can be used to monitor the PMO's perform-ance (e.g., status report, KPI, and audit process)

Leadership in a PMO

An organization's success in operating a PMO depends primarily on the competencies and the performance of its staff and most specifically on the hard and soft skills of the PMO's leader. The topic of leadership itself is a very broad one, and endless discussions on all types of leadership are in the market already. From those discussions, we have been able to draw some relevant concepts that we can apply to the PMO. This chapter begins with a brief discussion on leadership to get you familiar with the topic. We then describe the purpose that PMO leaders serve, examine the skills that effective PMO leaders should possess, and highlight the critical differences and key similarities between a PMO leader and a project leader.

The Role of a Leader

In an organizational context, leaders have the task of communicating the vision and mission of the company to its people, bringing the company to its final destination. Broadly speaking, organizational leaders fulfill three major roles (Carpenter and Sanders, 2009): interpersonal, informational, and decisional.

- Leaders perform *interpersonal roles:* as figureheads in performing ceremonial tasks, as liaisons to maintain relationships with external stakeholders, and as motivating leaders for internal stakeholders.

- *Informational roles* suggest the sharing of information with employees, monitoring, and being a spokesperson for outside stakeholders.

- In the *decisional roles*, leaders develop strategy, handle conflicts, negotiate, and allocate critical resources.

The Role of a PMO Leader

In an organizational context, leaders must possess or develop multiple skills to succeed. To understand the leadership role in a PMO, we need first to recognize the characteristics of a leader. Although there is no certain formula for what makes a good leader, leaders are commonly thought to have the following characteristics:

- Vision
- Listening skills
- Intelligence
- Decisiveness
- Ambition
- Negotiation skills
- Communication skills
- Physical stamina
- Courage to stand up for what they believe in
- Ability to make prompt judgments and take action
- Ability to motivate others
- Ability to adapt quickly in different environments
- Capability to live with the consequences of his or her decisions
- Strong ethical standards (trustworthiness)

These characteristics should make it clear that the scope of the leadership role includes that of management, and, of course, this prompts the old question of the difference between a manager and a leader. We can sum up the differences cited in the numerous debates on this question as follows:

- *Leaders* have a vision of where they want to bring the organization. To achieve that, they focus on the strategic direction of their charges and they empower and inspire them to reach that destination.

- *Managers,* on the other hand, focus on the logistics of "getting there": planning and budgeting, organizing the resources, and resolving the issues encountered in the company's day-to-day operation.

The role of the PMO leader is bestowed on anyone who takes the job title of PMO manager. Considering the leading and the managing aspects of the role, we can safely say that the PMO leader:

- Creates a vision for the PMO.

- Motivates the PMO members to move toward achieving that vision.

- Provides the necessary resources for the team.

- Embodies the group's values and principles.

- Guides the PMO team members in making decisions.

- Is the bond that unites the team.

- Creates a conducive environment for mutual trust.

- Represents the PMO in front of the project staff and business staff.

- Teaches other team members in liaising the two worlds (the project and the business).

Now that we know the characteristics required for a PMO leader and understand the role, the question to ask is, "What makes being a PMO leader unique among other leadership roles in the organization?" The answer to the question lies with the special set of skills required to be a PMO leader.

The Skills Required for PMO Leaders

A PMO strides between the project environment and the day-to-day business environment. As any books on project management explain, a project has a definite time frame, whereas a business operates continuously; thus a project manager (PM) and a general manager have different characteristics to suit their job requirements. The different characteristics translate to the requirements for an ideal PMO leader. In other words, considering the nature of a PMO, the leader must have the ability to work with people from both project and business environments and to appreciate how the two environments differ.

To sum up, a PMO manager must have the following skills and characteristics:

- *Project Skills and Business Skills.* Things are different in these two environments. For example, project finance has a different focus and methodology compared to day-to-day operational finance. A PMO manager must be able to understand the different methodologies used.

- *Communications Skills and People Skills to Bridge Both Worlds.* At times, a PMO manager will have to be a translator, or an arbiter, between project staff and business staff.

- *Ability to Envision How to Develop the PMO so That It Can Continuously Add Value to the Organization's Bottom Line.* The manager does this by always keeping abreast of the latest developments in project management and business strategy.

PMO Manager Versus Project Manager

Due to the relative newness of the PMO concept, the skills and role of a PMO manager are sometimes confused with those of a project

Making a Case for PMO: Selecting a Leader for PMO

After receiving a recommendation to establish a PMO from the management consulting firm Mackenzie & Co., Dave Strassen immediately went on a search for the best person to head this business unit. After three and a half months of searching, he had in front of him resumes from two very qualified people:

Rendy Strack was 45 years old with an MBA from a top university in Boston and was certified as a Project Management Professional (PMP). He had been a project manager for 20 years, and in the last five years, he had helped six companies get their PMOs off the ground.

Paul Witten was 43 years old with a master's degree in information technology from a top university in California. Also PMP certified, he had the same amount of project management experience as Rendy's. He'd helped a company on the West Coast set up a PMO about three years ago, and he had stayed with them as a PMO manager until he left recently because his wife wanted to move back to Boston.

Dave had an interview with both of them and agreed that they both hit it off with him. They were equally qualified for the job (sure, Paul had less experience in setting up a PMO, but his last company gave him a glowing recommendation on how wonderfully his PMO functions), and they both had the leadership qualities he was after. However, from his conversations with both of them, he began to lean toward picking Paul. Rendy was very good at setting up a PMO, but he'd be ready to move on to the next project as soon as his job was done. Paul, on the other hand, intended to stay with the company and run the PMO. Dave realized that other companies would probably pick Rendy, but Dave was after someone who wanted to stay with the PMO in the long term to build it. After thinking long and hard, he decided to give Paul the job as FAS's PMO manager.

manager (PM). Let's look at the critical similarities and the differences between the two.

Similarities

□   Both positions rely heavily on project management skills (i.e., completing projects on time, budget and scope, managing staffs, having the technical skills to use project management software, and so on).

□   Both managers must learn to tread the political water to achieve their project goals (i.e., competing with other projects for resource allocations, dealing with conflicts with various departmental managers impacted by their projects, and so on).

□   Both PMO managers and project managers are responsible for continuously improving the project management standard in their organization.

These striking similarities do not mean that the PMO manager's role is the same as the PM's.

Key Differences

□   A PMO manager is responsible for managing the office itself (i.e., staffing the PMO, training, developing a career path within the PMO, lobbying to gain funding for operating the PMO, and so on). A project manager is responsible for managing a particular project.

□   A PM ensures that the final product or service is delivered within the budget, on time, and of the specified quality, using the available resources allocated to the project. A PMO manager optimizes the use of available resources and allocates them differently according to the needs of the various projects.

- A PM can focus his/her attention on a single project. A PMO manager must be able to coordinate various projects at any one time, requiring a cross-functional perspective to understand how the different projects affect both the project environment and the business environment of the organization.

- In terms of specific tasks, the PMO manager is focused on devising optimum project management standards (thus saving the PMs from having to reinvent the wheel) and making sure they are implemented throughout the organization. The PM is responsible for adopting those standards for the particular project and providing feedback to the PMO if the standards need some updating.

- A PMO manager's job is a full-time position that is a part of the business's day-to-day operation. A PM's position (again, depending on the organizational structure discussed in Chapter 3) may be a temporary position that disappears when the project ends.

Conclusion

The similar roles of a PM and a PMO manager means that a project manager may be trained to be a good PMO manager and vice versa. However, because of the key differences, someone who is good as a project manager will not necessarily succeed in a PMO manager position. This is an important point to remember for someone who is selecting a PMO manager.

5 Things You Need to Remember from This Chapter

1. What leadership means to your organization

2. The necessary characteristics of a PMO leader

3. The role of a PMO leader

4. The skills required to lead a PMO

5. The similarities and differences between a PMO manager and a PM

Careers Within a PMO

The introduction of the PMO creates changes in the corporate structure, with related changes in job roles and opportunities within the company. Again, such change may worry some people. However, one way to positively communicate the benefits of having a PMO is by introducing the prospect for a career advancement within the PMO. This is an excellent way to drive acceptance of the PMO. In this chapter we will look at the natural progression of a project management career that is closely intertwined with the PMO and at the various staff needed to run a PMO.

A Project Management Career in the PMO

A defined project management career structure gives participants the opportunity to progress in their careers in a way not previously possible. It also contributes to the continuous improvement of the organization's project management capability because people will want to build on the skills required to facilitate their climb up the corporate ladder. Increasingly common are independent project career tracks within large corporations that previously would have been part of functional management responsibilities. Table 19.1 shows such a typical career track. As the position's responsibility increases, so does the contribution to the company's strategy and vision.

Those who decide on a project management career generally start out within a functional unit, taking on tasks within that area and managing them through to completion. Although they have responsibility for their business division, they would probably not be accountable for the overall deliverable. As the manager progresses up the career ladder, accountability and ownership of their projects become greater, as do the scope and complexity.

As the manager progresses, more responsibility is assigned, accompanied by greater visibility. To progress from level to level, it is recommended that the participant undertake formal training as well as building knowledge through experience. This will assist the PMO in its drive to become a center of excellence, teaching the people best practices and keeping them up-to-date with industry changes.

Staffing the PMO

The multifaceted role of a PMO requires multiskilled people to support the PMO manager. The staff must meet certain criteria, ranging from project management qualifications and experience to communication and negotiation skills. Although in general each staffer should possess the same characteristics as those of a PMO manager (as outlined in Chapter 18), the job functions require different skills. Considering the different roles and responsibilities a PMO has to take, in general, a PMO requires the following staff to ensure its successful operation:

Table 19.1 Typical Project Management Career Track

	Project Manager	Senior Project Manager	Director, Project Management	Vice President, Project Management
Role summary	• Manages projects of limited scope within functional reporting structure • Projects managed typically impact or require resource management within an individual department, functional in nature • Generally considered an individual contributor • Will contribute to solution approach • Requires minimal supervision • Operates within a functional team	• Manages one or more small to medium projects within functional reporting structure or business unit • Ownership and accountability for bringing project to fruition • Will require limited resource management within functional reporting structure or business unit • Will be responsible for approach to solutions • Requires no supervision • May have direct reports • Operates within a functional team	• Manages one or more highly complex technology projects or programs that span multiple areas and business functions • Prioritizes program/portfolio deliverables and is accountable for delivery • Projects managed require resource management across multiple functional areas and business units • Will develop standards and strategies to obtain desired results • Requires no supervision, will be called upon to participate in long-term strategic planning • Runs a team of project managers • May be part of the PMO	• Manages programs and/or project portfolios that are strategic in nature and will have a direct impact on the organization • Prioritizes program/portfolio deliverables and is accountable for delivery • Programs will impact organization as a whole and are generally focused on long-term results • Responsible for strategic planning • Communicates and drives business mission • Has decision-making authority in relation to budgets, resources, technical strategies, processes for delivery, etc. • Runs a team of project or portfolio managers • Member of senior or executive management team • Runs PMO or on senior team

Making a Case for PMO: The PMO and Career Tracks

Two years after its inception, the PMO at FAS Inc. was thriving. It was gaining acceptance and respect from the organization, and as a result its scope of work was getting bigger as people start to trust the PMO more with their projects. Paul Witten, the PMO manager, had been needing assistance to do his job. So far, he'd been getting temporary project managers and support staff from within the company, but they always had to go back to their seconding departments. In the meantime, he'd been talking to various people within the organization who were interested in pursuing a project management career. Some of them had had the experience of managing small projects in their departments, but project management was not exactly their job responsibility. Some others, mostly in the IT department, had been managing projects for years; in fact, a lot of the IT staff were project managers before they came onboard. Meanwhile, the rest had no project management experience whatsoever but were very interested in getting one. On Paul's initiative, FAS Inc. had been providing some short project management courses, but then he realized that he could do more: "Considering all these interests, why not build a career track out of the PMO?"

In discussion with Charlene Wincott, the head of the HR department, they started toying with the idea. They agreed that the PMO was ripe for expansion and that it needed skillful permanent staff. So they created openings within the PMO for an analyst position, a technical position, and an administrative position. They realized that these positions could provide functional staff (e.g., the accountants, the IT programmers, and the like) with a bridge to a project management career, and they could also provide opportunities for project managers to diversify their project management experience. Once they got the approval from the CEO, the PMO was set on its way to becoming a career path. That's how the FAS's PMO became the fully functioning PMO we know today.

PMO Manager

- The manager's main responsibility is to establish strategic direction for the PMO. The strategy should be closely aligned with the organization's overall direction, while creating a competitive advantage for the PMO.

- The manager is responsible for overseeing the PMO operation and its staff performance, while developing good working relationships with clients and stakeholders to fulfill business needs.

- The manager ensures that business objectives are accomplished through the successful completion of projects. The PMO manager must therefore have a high-level overview of all projects' performance, in order to provide reliable advice to senior executives in making business decisions. In other words, the PMO manager should be able to demonstrate a capability to manage the PMO as an independent business unit that adds value to the whole organization.

PMO IT Staff

It is important to note that the PMO should be proficient not only in project management, but also in IT-related matters. Considering that almost all projects initiated in a modern organization require IT involvement, these technology staff are valuable resources in the creation of an advantageous position for the PMO, especially in projects where IT-related matters are the main issues.

PMO IT staffs are expected to integrate their technical knowledge into the project management environment. This role may include representing the PMO in providing technical opinions, as well as providing technical services to the PMO itself.

PMO Analyst

The role of a PMO analyst is to assist the PMO manager in the creation of a project management environment that follows a best practice standard. A PMO analyst's tasks include the following:

- Development, implementation, and management of project management processes and procedures

- Conducting various project management–related research to improve the organization's project management practice

- Assisting the PMO manager with project audit exercises

- Assisting the PMO manager with monitoring project performance in terms of cost, schedule, and resource utilization

- Providing analysis reports on the PMO's performance (i.e., analysis of the PMO's budget, revenue, expenditure, and so on)

- Organizing project management training and certification

The project analyst is expected to be a generalist with a variety of knowledge and experience in multiple fields, from finance to IT. This background enables the analyst to be nimble in moving among projects and across functional departments.

PMO Administration Staff

Depending on the organization's capacity and funding availability, sometimes the roles of a PMO administration staff and a PMO analyst are carried out by the same person. However, it is important to draw the distinction between the two and realize that the role of an administrator must not be diminished if the PMO's smooth operation is to be guaranteed. A PMO administrator's tasks may include the following:

- Liaising with various project managers to compile recurring project management progress reports and other documents for regular project committee review

- Organizing the distribution of information from the PMO to all project offices

- Coordinating project management learning and development activities in collaboration with the HR department

- Providing administrative support, such as filing, archiving, and photocopying

For all of these roles, potential candidates have to meet the following selection criteria:

- *Academic Qualification:* This may include diplomas, degrees, or other certification that equips candidates with complete knowledge and training to fulfill their roles.

- *Relevant Experience:* Candidates must demonstrate some hands-on capability and experience in accomplishing similar roles. When such experience is lacking, recruiters must determine a candidate's potential to learn on the job.

- *Understanding of Business Operation:* Candidates must have an understanding and appreciation for the organization's core business to ensure their ability to contribute to the overall business aims.

- *Understanding of Project Management Concept:* All candidates should have a broad and deep understanding of project management principles and their methods, to enable them to effectively work in the PMO.

Conclusion

An organization that is committed to improving its project management capabilities should consider developing an independent project
management career track within a PMO. Establishing such a career
development avenue will not only contribute to the skills advancement for the PMO, but also create a stepping stone for the staff to
begin a career in project management. The benefits of the career
track will be increased acceptance for the PMO and overall career
satisfaction that is organizationwide.

5 Things You Need to Remember from This Chapter

1. The possibility of developing a PMO as an avenue for staff
   to build their careers

2. How an organization can ensure that the staff's project
   management careers and experience grow by adding
   progressively more responsibilities

3. The various positions available in a PMO

4. The responsibilities associated with each position

5. The selection criteria for PMO staff (academic
   qualifications, relevant project management experience,
   understanding of how the company operates, and so on)

PART V

CONCLUSION

Final Thoughts on PMO

As we near the end of our mission of introducing the concept of PMO to a wide-ranging audience, we conclude the book by briefly reviewing today's PMO (How do organizations perceive it? How is its implementation across different companies?) and the broader future of PMO (Will a PMO have a place in organizations? Will the use of PMO become widely accepted? How will it be shaped and run to suit future business challenges?). After reviewing the varying research papers (like the ones discussed in this chapter) and the differing opinions from project management experts, the authors believe that the use of PMO will become more and more common in the future and that the future PMO will have a greater role in steering organizations' strategy.

Today's Program Management Office

Studies regarding the existing practice of the PMO within large organizations are largely ambivalent about their effectiveness. The 2007 study undertaken for the Project Management Institute (PMI) by Dr. Brian J. Hobbs, "The Multi-Project PMO: A Global Analysis of the

Current State of Practice," notes that, at the moment, there is a wide variation in PMO implementation, in their perceived effectiveness, and in their roles within the organization. A key finding is "Lack of Consensus in the Value of PMOs." The PMI study and other discussions on the effectiveness of the office note that 50 percent of the companies screened value the PMO and 50 percent challenge its legitimacy.

However, in another survey conducted by *CIO* magazine and the PMI,* survey respondents reported positive benefits from the formation of a PMO, even if quantifiable return on investment is elusive. Out of the 450 people surveyed, 303 (67 percent) said their companies have a PMO. Of those with a PMO, half said the PMO has improved project success rates, 22 percent didn't know or don't track that metric, and 16 percent said success rates stayed the same. It is also important to note that there is also a strong link between the length of time a PMO has been operating and project success rates: the longer the better. Whereas 37 percent of those who have had a PMO for less than one year reported increased success rates, those with a PMO operating for more than four years reported a 65 percent success rate increase. The top two reasons for establishing a PMO, according to the survey: improving project success rates and implementing standard practices.

The Future of the Program Management Office

So how do these findings affect the future of the PMO? Although the current general perception is split evenly between the believers and the cynics, corporate leaders are increasingly investing in project management best practices as a methodology for delivering return

---

*Megan Santosus, "Why You Need a Project Management Office," *CIO*, July 2003, http://www.cio.com/article/29887/Why_You_Need_a_Project_Management_Office_PMO_.

on investment for projects. KPMG's 2005 research, "Global IT Project Management Survey," noted that senior management teams are being held accountable for benefits derived from investment and that the benefit is realized in the form of successful project output.

The same survey also noted that organizations that are more successful than their competitors generally have good project governance processes in place. Twenty-two percent of those companies noted that their Program Management Offices are responsible for managing all projects within the organization, and 30 percent had PMOs that reported directly to the board on the projects' status.

Paradoxically, there is a belief that, although the PMO is seen by some as ineffective, the majority of organizations believe that some form of governance and formalized project management is required to realize a return on project investment. The more successful organizations utilize the PMO as a central hub for project execution, and these PMOs are viewed favorably by their companies. Based on these findings, it can be extrapolated that mature PMOs that employ experienced and knowledgeable staff are much more likely to succeed than those that do not.

As corporations look to benefits realized from project undertakings as a way to drive their organizational goals, the role of the PMO can only gain in prevalence. Corporate boards' focus on results from project investment, the number of actions undertaken, and the processes put in place to support the projects is resulting in a growth in operations' complexity that requires careful oversight and control.

Indeed, the Project Management Institute's introduction of its Global Standard for Program Management is a recognition of the complexity and increased predominance of the practice. Thus, as program management becomes more widespread, the need for standardized best practice within an organization will increase. In other words, the PMO will not only be more widely accepted, it will also have a more dominant role in the planning and execution of the corporate vision in the future. *[It is important to note that such a trend may translate to an increased reliance on technology and corporate governance to facilitate the stakeholders and project teams who are becoming more dispersed geographically and the greater demand for real-time responses from the PMO.]*

The reality of the modern economy is posing new challenges as companies are increasingly struggling to organize, manage, and track projects. The pressure is on to deliver less expensive but high-quality projects in a short period of time with limited resources. The continuously changing dynamics result in creeping project scope, increase of risk, scarcity of resources, and increasing project interdependence. All of these would require a new approach that is encapsulated in a PMO. We hope that after reading this book, our readers will be inspired to investigate how the PMO can help improve the competitive advantage of their organizations.

APPENDICES

PMO Business Plan

COMPANY ABC

Sample PMO Business Plan
Revision Date: _____

Document Owners

PMO Manager	Joe Blog; email: jb@joeblog.com; ph: xxx-xxx-xxxx
PMO Analyst	Jane Doe; email: jd@joeblog.com; ph: xxx-xxx-xxxx

Document History

Document Revision/Release Status

Revision	Date	Description	Author/Editor
0.1	02/15/09	First Draft	Joe Blog
0.2	04/15/09	Second Draft	Joe Blog
0.3	06/15/09	Third Draft	Jane Doe
0.4	08/15/09	Fourth Draft	Joe Blog
1.0	10/15/09	First Approved	Joe Blog

Document Distribution

Name	Required	Title	E-mail	Phone
A	Approve	CEO		
B	Approve	Director of Finance Department		
C	Approve	Director of IT Department		
D	Review	Senior Project Manager		
E	Review	Project Officer		

Background

After taking into consideration the numerous opportunities presented by the current business environment and the company's existing project capabilities, we would like to propose a Program Management Office (PMO).

The current market provides business opportunities that translate to project activities. With numerous projects running at the same time, the company needs some coordination to ensure not only that we select the best projects, but also that we implement them efficiently (in terms of cost savings, better management of projects' risks, higher quality of deliverables, and so on).

The coordination can be met through the creation of a Program Management Office. The following Business Plan outlines the benefits of having a PMO as well as the amount of funding and resources required.

PMO Objectives Summary

We aim to achieve the following objectives through the implementation of a PMO *[Note: It is important to be as detailed as possible when outlining an objective; that is, include when the objective will be achieved, what will be required to achieve it, and so on.]*

Objectives	Time Frame
Have the ability to coordinate the project resources and allocate them according to priorities.	6 months from PMO inception
Implement standardized methodology, processes, and tools, thus allowing a consistent measure between each project's success.	3 months within PMO inception
Establish flexible flow of information between project participants and the rest of the company.	1 month within PMO inception
Improving the company's project management capabilities through mentoring, training, and so on.	Within 2 months of PMO inception
Create a methodology that allows for better selection of projects that serve the company's mission and vision.	Within 1 month of PMO inception

PMO Activities (Roles and Responsibilities)

To meet those objectives, we envision the PMO's carrying out the following activities:

- Assisting projects by managing resources, customers, and vendors

- Conducting project audits to identify any areas for future improvements or to put projects back on track

- Monitoring the program's progress, including its financial status, quality, deliverables, and so on

- Providing project management training, while introducing standardized methods, processes, templates

- Creating a project selection method and continuously improving it

- Conducting project audits

- Conducting knowledge management by creating a repository to retain information and ensure that relevant staff have the right level of access

  ◻ Managing the flow of communication and information between the project and business environments

PMO Management

We understand that one of the most important factors in ensuring the success of the PMO is excellent management. As a result, working together with the HR department, we have decided to select Mr. James Spelling, with his 20 years of experience in project management (including six years as a PMO manager), to be our PMO manager. He will be assisted by a PMO analyst and a PMO coordinator. All of the PMO staff will be selected based on their project management skills, knowledge, and experience (specifically in the PMO area).

Resources Requested

Upon review, the following resources will be needed to ensure the smooth operation of the PMO:

  ◻ Office space

  ◻ Communication equipment (telephone, fax machine, and the like)

  ◻ Computer (with supporting software and adequate hardware)

Financial Analysis

We also have conducted a Cost-Benefit Analysis, which shows that the PMO will bring positive financial impacts to the company. The summary calculation of the analysis is presented in the following table. It presents a five-year estimated future cash flow (including the intangible benefits) discounted to present value. A more detailed calculation will be presented upon request. *[Note: A brief overview of Cost-Benefit Analysis can be found in Chapter 2.]*

Benefits

1. Yearly savings from approving the "wrong" projects $300,000

2. Increased revenue from having standardized
   project management processes $190,000

3. Yearly savings from project costs that can be
   avoided by having a PMO $80,000

4. Increased revenue from improving staff's project
   management skills $50,000

Costs

1. Yearly PMO staff's salaries $350,000

2. Yearly equipment and space rental and purchase $50,000

3. Yearly PMO training $50,000

Assuming all the benefits and costs occur at time 0, the net income for the organization is $620,000 – $450,000 = $170,000. The increased revenue per year thus justifies the PMO establishment.

Conclusion

To take advantage of the opportunities currently offered by the market, the company has to run multiple projects at the same time. As discussed in this business plan, the existence of a PMO will provide us with numerous benefits. On top of that, the Cost-Benefit Analysis we conducted indicates that the investment in a PMO will pay for itself while presenting positive returns to the company, further justifying its presence. Thus, we strongly recommend the establishment of a PMO.

Sample Project Office Templates

Work Breakdown Structure Package

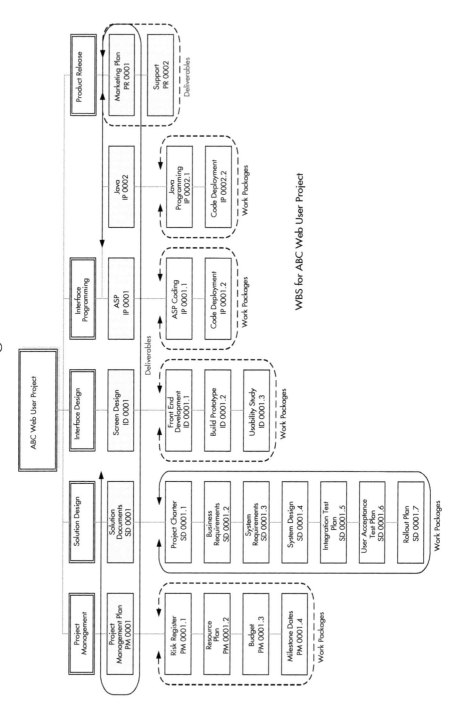

WBS for ABC Web User Project

Deliverables Register

Reference Number	Deliverables	Assigned to	Deadline	Status (Date)	Approving Stakeholder(s)
PM 0001.1	Risk Management Plan • Risk Register • Risk Breakdown • Mitigation Plan	Business	August 8, 2007	Ongoing	Project Director
PM 0001.2	Resource Plan	Project Manager	August 8, 2007	Ongoing	Project Manager and Project Director
PM 0001.3	Budget • Cost Estimates • Market Data	Financial Analyst	September 8, 2007	Input PM 0001.2	Project Manager and Project Director
PM 0001.4	Milestone Dates	Project Manager	November 15, 2007	Input PM 0001.1 PM 0001.2 PM 0001.3	Steering Committee

Issue Register

Reference Number	Issue	Priority (H/M/L)	Identified By	Status (Open/Closed)	Issue Owner (Action Required)
Issue Category 1: Human Resource					
1.1	Holiday season was not taken into account in Project Plan, resulting in possible late delivery of IT Requirement document	Medium	IT Analyst	Open. Raised at Status Meeting on April 7, 2007.	IT Analyst
Issue Category 2: Cost					
2.1	Higher cost than initial estimate to engage software vendor due to lack of tender participants	High	IT Analyst	Closed. Steering Committee approved higher budget on May 9, 2007.	Project Manager
Issue Category 3: Schedule					
3.1					

Risk Register

Reference Number	Risk	Probability (H/M/L)	Impact (H/M/L)	Identified By	Status (Open/Closed)	Risk Owner (Action Required)
Risk Category 1: Human Resource						
1.1	Possible workers' strike in June, which may impact the project completion date	Medium	Medium	Project Manager	Closed. Approval has been obtained from Project Director to engage contractors during strike day.	Project Manager
Risk Category 2: Cost						
2.1	The limited number of highly skilled specialized vendors may result in higher cost than estimated	High	High	IT Analyst	Opened. Raised at Steering Committee Meeting on May 9, 2007.	Project Manager
Risk Category 3: Schedule						
3.1						

Change Register

Reference Number	Change	Requested by	Status (Open/Closed)	Change Owner (Action Required)
Change Category 1: Project Management				
1.1	Weekly status meeting to be changed from every Thursday 1:00 p.m. to every Friday 1:00 p.m. to better accommodate all participants	Project Manager	Closed. Approved by Project Director on June 23, 2009.	Project Manager
Change Category 2: Cost				
2.1				
Change Category 3: Schedule				
3.1				

Project Finance Record

Project Name: Sample Project
For the Financial Year: 2009/2010

Project Revenue

Item	Jul-09	Aug-09	Sep-09	Oct-09	Nov-09	Dec-09	Jan-09	Feb-09	Mar-09	Apr-09	May-09	Jun-09	Total
	$000	$000	$000	$000	$000	$000	$000	$000	$000	$000	$000	$000	$000
Payment from client	8	9	5	14	2	1	3	7	9	6	4	0	68

Project Expenditure

Item	Jul-09	Aug-09	Sep-09	Oct-09	Nov-09	Dec-09	Jan-09	Feb-09	Mar-09	Apr-09	May-09	Jun-09	Total
	$000	$000	$000	$000	$000	$000	$000	$000	$000	$000	$000	$000	$000
Payment to Vendor													
Printing Cost													

Comment: _____

Project Status Report

Project Name: Sample Project

Date: _____

Item	Actual to Date	Project Plan	Status (Green/Red/Amber)*	Item Owner
Payment to Vendors	$10,000	$15,000	Green	Project Manager
Financial Analysis Report	50% complete	70% complete	Amber	Financial Analyst
Business Information Report	20% complete	70% complete	Red	BIR Analyst

Number of variations requested to date: _____

Actions achieved since last Status Report:

_____

_____

Forward actions:

_____

_____

Key decisions made:

_____

_____

* Status indications:

Green—Item's progress is on track.

Amber—Item might be off-track and corrective actions may be needed.

Red—Corrective actions to be taken immediately.

Sample PMO Charter

COMPANY ABC

Sample PMO Charter

Revision Date: _____

Document Owners

PMO Manager   Joe Blog; email: jb@joeblog.com; ph: xxx-xxx-xxxx

PMO Analyst   Jane Doe; email: jd@joeblog.com; ph: xxx-xxx-xxxx

Document History

Document Revision/Release Status

Revision	Date	Description	Author/Editor
0.1	02/15/09	First Draft	Joe Blog
0.2	04/15/09	Second Draft	Joe Blog
0.3	06/15/09	Third Draft	Jane Doe
0.4	08/15/09	Fourth Draft	Joe Blog
1.0	10/15/09	First Approved	Joe Blog

Document Distribution

Name	Required	Title	E-mail	Phone
A	Approve	CEO		
B	Approve	Director of Finance Department		
C	Approve	Director of IT Department		
D	Review	Senior Project Manager		
E	Review	Project Officer		

The Program Management Office (PMO) was established to improve ABC Company's project management capability and the Company's competitive advantage. To enable the PMO to provide independent services, the PMO will operate as a separate division reporting directly to the CEO. This PMO Charter outlines the PMO's vision and mission, responsibilities, strategies, key stakeholders, and critical success factors.

PMO Vision and Mission

The PMO's vision is to position the company to be the benchmark in its industry. By continually improving the company's project management capability, the PMO directly takes part in expanding the company's competitive advantage.

The PMO's mission is to provide leadership to the project management providers within the Company (project managers, project analysts, and other project team members), enabling them to work in an efficient and effective project environment (i.e., through standardization of methodologies, provision of tools, risk management, and so on) and thus helping them to produce project deliverables within the agreed schedules, budgets, and quality standards.

PMO Objectives

In support of those objectives, here are the PMO's primary tasks:

- Facilitate coordination between the project group and the business group to ensure that all undertaken projects are aligned with the company's business objectives.

- Improve the project management practice within the company in order to achieve the monetary benefits (e.g., through project cost savings, reduce exposure to project failures, and so on) and quality project outcomes.

- Manage project resources (human resources, information, facilities, and so on) to ensure optimized use of them.

PMO Responsibilities

To meet those objectives, the PMO is given the following responsibilities: *[Note: The outline of the PMO's responsibilities in the charter should be as detailed as possible. The following examples serve as a general guideline in the areas of functionality to be included in the charter.]*

- Developing structured project management training for both project and business staff

- Working with the business executives, assisting with project selection and project audit at the end of a project

- Standardizing the company's project management methodology, processes and procedures, and tools

- Managing the flow and repository of information and knowledge, and ensuring that relevant staff have the right level of access

- Monitoring the program and alerting the relevant project executives when a certain project is going off track

- Assisting projects with vendor management and customer management

PMO Strategies

To ensure that the PMO can achieve its mission and vision, the support from key stakeholders and end users is very important. The following is an outline of the PMO's strategies to achieve those supports:

- Circulate the PMO Charter to obtain inputs from key stakeholders, and ensure that all relevant parties are consulted (especially on matters that are subject to differing opinions such as on project metrics, project selection criteria, and the PMO's key performance indicators).
- Refine the PMO Charter based on those inputs.
- Have the approval of the relevant executives on the PMO Charter.
- Establish an iterative review and update process for the PMO Charter.

PMO Critical Success Factors

Looking at the PMO from multiple angles and the key players involved, it is obvious that a lot of factors are critical to the success of the PMO, such as the ones outlined in the following examples:

- Executive support to enable the PMO to leverage the industry's best practice
- End user support and involvement (to facilitate a change-receptive environment that will be crucial when implementing the PMO)
- Provision of capable resources
- Provision of sufficient funding
- Agreement on the PMO's authorities and responsibilities
- Agreement on the key measures of the PMO's success
- Communication that flows both ways: to project executives and to end users

In addition to those success factors, we also have identified the following as barriers to success:

-   The perception that the PMO is the silver bullet solution to all of the company's business problems
-   The expectation of the PMO to deliver a quick fix when, in fact, some of the problems require long-term solutions
-   Viewing the PMO as an overhead (cost center) instead of a profit center
-   Office politics that result in the PMO's being considered a threat
-   Limited funding and resources

PMO Escalation Model

When project issues cannot be resolved within the project itself, even with the assistance of the PMO, the PMO will facilitate the escalation of the issues to higher authorities. The escalation process ensures that the relevant authorities are informed within a specific time frame to ensure a timely solution. The escalation path will follow this model:

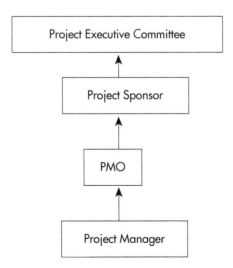

The project issues will be escalated only if it cannot be resolved by the lowest level of authority, and the PMO will be involved in every escalation step.

PMO Key Stakeholders

The PMO regards the following as primary stakeholders:

CEO	PMO Sponsor	• Ensures that the PMO has the necessary resources and funding for optimum operation • Resolves issues related to the PMO • Approves PMO's initiatives
Project Executive Committee	Project Sponsor	• Resolves project issues • Provides project directions • Approves project deliverables • Approves project funding • Approves project time frame • Reviews project's alignment with business' goals
Project Managers	Project Subject Matter Expert (SME)	• Ensures project compliance with PMO's project management standards • Ensures timely delivery of project goals • Escalates project issues when they cannot be resolved within the project • Ensures flow of communication with the PMO
Project Officers	Project Subject Matter Expert (SME)	• Assists the project managers with project completion
Department Heads	Client	• Ensures effective communication of the expectations within the PMO • Supports the PMO when dealing with projects taking place in the department
Business Staff	End Users	• Provides feedback on PMO services • Is actively involved when required by the PMO

PMO Organizational Structure

The PMO will report directly to the CEO. By operating independently, it is expected that the PMO will be able to provide an unbiased service to other departments within the organization.

```
                        ┌─────────┐
                        │   CEO   │
                        └─────────┘
        ┌───────────────┬─────────┴─────────┬───────────────┐
┌───────────────┐ ┌───────────┐   ┌───────────┐   ┌───────────┐
│   Program     │ │  Finance  │   │   Legal   │   │    HR     │
│  Management   │ │ Department│   │ Department│   │ Department│
│    Office     │ │           │   │           │   │           │
└───────────────┘ └───────────┘   └───────────┘   └───────────┘
```

This charter is a living document that will be continuously reviewed and updated as circumstances and project management capabilities evolve.

Signed:_____   Signed: _____

_____   _____

Date: _____   Date: _____

Joe Blog   Andrew Guy
PMO Manager   CEO
ABC Company   ABC Company

Sample PMO
Integration Plan

COMPANY ABC

PMO Integration Plan

Revision Date: _____

Document Owners

PMO Manager	Joe Blog; email: jb@joeblog.com; ph: xxx-xxx-xxxx
PMO Analyst	Jane Doe; email: jd@joeblog.com; ph: xxx-xxx-xxxx

Document History

Document Revision/Release Status

Revision	Date	Description	Author/Editor
0.1	02/15/09	First Draft	Joe Blog
0.2	04/15/09	Second Draft	Joe Blog
0.3	06/15/09	Third Draft	Jane Doe
0.4	08/15/09	Fourth Draft	Joe Blog
1.0	10/15/09	First Approved	Joe Blog

Document Distribution

Name	Required	Title	E-mail	Phone
A	Approve	CEO		
B	Approve	Director of Finance Department		
C	Approve	Director of IT Department		
D	Review	Senior Project Manager		
E	Review	Project Officer		

Introduction

This PMO Integration Plan has been developed to assist the PMO proponents to seamlessly integrate the PMO into the organization. It outlines the various activities that will take place, persons in charge, and estimated timelines and costs, to ensure that every activity is carried out within the agreed time frame and cost. This document is also created to capture the support of PMO sponsors, encouraging buy-in from other stakeholders.

PMO Implementation Team:

PMO Sponsor:

Date:

Change Reason

[Outline here the reason for the change, the benefits for the change, and the possible consequences of status quo.]

Integration Scope

[Describe here what will be involved and required in the integration process in terms of people, systems, processes, facilities, and other resources (i.e., where the PMO staff will be located, what facilities will be required, how this will affect other staff, and so on).]

Existing Environment

[Outline here the organization's current project management capabilities, available resources, staff's readiness for a change, staff's expected responses, and so on. An analysis of the key stakeholders is also required (sample at end of the appendix).]

Future Environment

[Describe here the desired environment (e.g., more effective project management tools, more efficient interaction between the project entities and the business entities, and so on).]

Action Plan

[From an analysis of the current situation and the future (or desired) environment, outline here the activities that will be required to successfully implement the PMO (sample at end of the appendix). Address various aspects such as people, systems, processes, resources, etc.]

Communication Plan

[The communication plan should outline how the changes will be communicated, the audience, the frequency of communication, and so on (sample at end of the appendix).]

Management Plan

[It is important to think about risk management in the PMO integration plan. Potential risks, such as the possibility of staff resistance, budget overflow, and the like, should be identified, and mitigating actions should be planned.]

Monitoring and Evaluation

The integration process will be constantly monitored through established communication channels (e.g., forums, e-mail, surveys, etc.). The PMO committee will regularly review the feedbacks and take the necessary corrective actions to ensure that the PMO is integrated into the organization seamlessly and supported by the staff.

Signed:_____   Signed: _____

_____   _____

Date: _____   Date: _____

Joe Blog   Andrew Guy
PMO Manager   CEO
ABC Company   ABC Company

Sample Action Plan

Activity	Person in Charge	Duration	Start/End Date	Estimated Cost	Resources
Conduct key stakeholders analysis					
Brief staff on the changes about to take place					
Conduct a survey of staff's response					
Analyze survey					
Conduct a workshop with staff to identify possible improvements on implementation plan					
Identify resources to acquire					

Sample Key Stakeholders Analysis

Stakeholder	Role	Interests	Communication Methods	Possible Conflict
Project managers	PMO's clients	• Improved project management methodologies and tools • Access to a centralized repository of project management knowledge	• Weekly meeting with project managers • Monthly newsletters	PM conflicting interests on project ranking and selection method

Sample Communication Plan

Audience	Key Message	Delivery Method	Communication Frequency	Date
Project managers	• Staged changes to project management tools and methodology to be adopted organizationwide	• Training forum • Newsletters • E-mails	• Intensive 2-week training, followed by quarterly training to keep the PMs' skills up-to-date • Weekly newsletter informing the audience of progress • Ad hoc e-mail communication	

References

Amason, Allen C., Zvi Aronson, Peter Dominick, Patricia Holahan, Thomas Lechler, Ann Mooney, Richard R. Reilly, and Aaron J. Shenhar. "The Human Side of Project Leadership." Newtown, Penn.: Project Management Institute, 2008.

Barlett, C. *McKinsey and Company: Managing Knowledge and Learning.* Case no. 9–396–357. Boston: Harvard Business School, 1996.

Barney, J. B. "Firm Resources and Sustained Competitive Advantage." *Journal of Management* 17:1 (1991): 99–121.

Bettger, Frank. *How I Raised Myself from Failure to Success in Selling.* New York: Simon & Schuster, 1947 (reprinted 1992).

Bourgault, Mario, and Natalie Drouin. "How's Your Distributed Team Doing? 10 Suggestions from the Field." Newtown, Penn.: Project Management Institute, 2007.

Brown, James T. *The Handbook of Program Management: How to Facilitate Project Success with Optimal Program Management.* New York: McGraw-Hill, 2007.

Carpenter, M. A., and W. G. Sanders. *Strategic Management.* Upper Saddle River, N.J.: Pearson-Prentice Hall, 2009.

Chandler, Neil. "Analytic Applications: Buy vs. Build vs. Customize" (Gartner Research G00152707). Stamford, Conn.: Gartner Research, November 2, 2007.

Clampitt, Phillip G. *Communicating for Managerial Effectiveness*, 2nd ed. Thousand Oaks, Calif.: Sage Publications, 2001.

Coff, R. W. "Human Assets and Management Dilemmas: Coping with Hazards on the Road to Resource-Based Theory." *Academy of Management Review* 22 (1997): 374–402.

Collins, Gem. *Thesaurus*, 3rd ed. New York: HarperCollins, 2005.

Collins, J. *Good to Great: Why Some Companies Make the Leap . . . and Others Don't*. New York: HarperBusiness, 2001.

Covey, Stephen R. *The 7 Habits of Highly Effective People*. New York: Simon & Schuster, 1989.

Daft, R. L. *Management,* 6th ed. New York: Southwestern, 2003.

DiMaggio, P. J., and W. Powell. "The Iron Cage Revisited: Institutional Isomorphism and Collective Rationality in Organizational Fields." *American Sociological Review* 48 (1983): 147–160.

Drucker, Peter. *The Age of Discontinuity*. Edison, N.J.: Transaction Publishers, 1992.

Duggal, Jack S. "Centralizing PMOs: What to Watch Out for and What You Should Know." Project Management Institute Community Post, September 2008, http://www.pmi.org/eNews/Post/2008_09-12/NLU_CentralizingPMOsWhatToWatchOutForWhatToKnow.html.

Frame, J. Davidson. *Project Management Competence*. San Francisco: Jossey-Bass, 1999.

Gartner Research. "The Project Office: Teams, Processes, Tools." Stamford, Conn.: Gartner Research, 2003.

Grant, R. *Contemporary Strategy Analysis*. Malden, Mass.: Blackwell Publishing, 2008.

Greenberg, P. *CRM at the Speed of Light: Essential Customer Strategies for the 21st Century*, 3rd ed. New York: McGraw-Hill, 2004.

Hambrick, D., and A. Canella. "Strategy Implementation as Substance and Selling." *Academy of Management Executive* 3:4 (1989): 278–285.

Hamel, G., and C. K. Prahalad. *Competing for the Future*. Boston: Harvard Business School Press, 1994.

Hannan, M. T., L. Pollos, and G. R. Carroll. "Structural Inertia and Organizational Change Revisited III: The Evolution of Organizational Inertia." Stanford GSB Research Paper 1734 (April 2002).

Hrebiniak, L. G., and W. Joyce. *Implementing Strategy*. New York: Macmillan, 1984.

Hobbs, Brian. "The Multi-Project PMO: A Global Analysis of the Current State of Practice" (white paper). Newtown, Penn.: Project Management Institute, 2007.

Imhoff, Claudia. "The Role of Program Management for BI," *Executive Update* 2:16 (2002).

Jick, T. D., and M. A. Peiperl. *Managing Change*. Boston: McGraw Hill-Irwin, 2003.

Kaplan, R., and D. Norton. *The Strategy-Focused Organization*. Boston: Harvard Business School Press, 2001.

Kaplan, R. S., and D. P. Norton. *Balanced Scorecard: Translating Strategy into Action*. Boston: Harvard Business School Press, 1996.

Kaplan, R. S., and D. P. Norton. "The Balanced Scorecard: Measures that Drive Performance." *Harvard Business Review*, Best of HBR (2005): 172–180.

Kerzner, Harold. *Project Management: A Systems Approach to Planning, Scheduling and Controlling*, 8th ed. Hoboken, N.J.: John Wiley & Sons, 2003.

Kotter, John. *Leading Change*. Boston: Harvard Business School Press, 1996.

Leonard-Barton, D. "Core Capabilities and Core Rigidities: A Paradox in Managing New Product Development." *Strategic Management Journal*, Summer Special Issue (1992): 111–125.

Light, Matt, and Daniel B Stang. "Magic Quadrant for IT Project and Portfolio Management, 2007" (Gartner Research Note G00149082). Stamford, Conn.: Gartner Research, 2007.

March, J. G. "Exploration and Exploitation in Organizational Learning." *Organization Science* 2 (1991): 71–87.

Melik, Rudolf. *The Rise of the Project Workforce: Managing Projects and People in a Flat World*. Hoboken, N.J.: John Wiley & Sons, 2007.

Menon, Nita. *Passion at the Workplace*. Newtown, Penn.: Project Management Institute, 2008.

Milgrom, P. R., and J. Roberts. "Complementarities and Fit: Strategy, Structure, and Organizational Change in Manufacturing." *Journal of Accounting and Economics* 19 (1995): 179–208.

Mullaly, Mark. *The Multiplicity of PMOs*. June 2008, Gantthead.com.

———. *The Four Archetypes of the PMO*. June 2002, Gantthead.com.

Office of Government Commerce. *The Centre of Excellence Pocketbook*. London: Office of Government Commerce, 2006, http://www.ogc.gov.uk/documents/TheCentreOfExcellencePocketbook.pdf.

Porter, M. *Competitive Strategy*. New York: Free Press, 1980.

Porter, M. E., and N. Siggelkow. "Contextual Interactions Within Activity Systems and Sustainable Competitive Advantage" (working paper). Boston: Harvard Business School, 2002.

Project Management Institute. *A Guide to the Project Management Body of Knowledge*, 3rd ed. Newtown, Penn.: Project Management Institute, 2004.

Project Management Institute. *The Standard for Program Management*. Newtown, Penn.: Project Management Institute, 2006.

Pugh, Katrina, and Nancy M. Dixon. "Don't Just Capture Knowledge, Put It to Work," *Harvard Business Review* (May 1, 2008).

———. "Harvesting Process Knowledge. NASA," *ASK* (Spring 2008).

Romanelli, E., and M. L. Tushman. "Organizational Transformation as Punctuated Equilibrium: An Empirical Test." *Academy of Management Journal* 37 (1994): 1141–1166.

Santosus, M. "Why You Need a Project Management Office." *CIO* (July 2003), http://www.cio.com/article/29887/Why_You_Need_a_Project_Management_Office_PMO_.

Schein, E. H. "Organizational Culture." *American Psychologist* 45 (1990): 109–119.

Shani, A. B., and J. A. Sena. "Information Technology and the Integration of Change: A Sociotechnical Systems Approach." *Journal of Applied Behavioral Science* 30 (1994): 247–270.

Shenhar, Aaron J., and Dov Dvir. *Reinventing Project Management: The Diamond Approach to Successful Growth and Innovation*. Boston: Harvard Business School Press, 2007.

Soodek, Andy. *PPM Tool Selection and Implementation Considerations*. Newtown, Penn.: Project Management Institute, 2008.

Spender, J. C. *Industry Recipes*. Oxford: Blackwell, 1989.

Thomas, Janice, and Mark Mullaly. *Researching the Value of Project Management*. Newtown, Penn.: Project Management Institute, 2007.

Trist, E. "The Sociotechnical Perspective." In Andrew H. Van de Ven and William F. Joyce (eds.), *Perspectives on Organization Design and Behavior*. Hoboken, N.J.: John Wiley & Sons, 1984.

Turner, J. Rodney, Martina Hueman, and Anne Keegan. *Human Resource Management in the Project-Oriented Organization.* Newtown, Penn.: Project Management Institute, 2008.

Tushman, M. L., and E. Romanelli. "Organizational Evolution: A Metamorphosis Model of Convergence and Reorientation." In L. L. Cummins and B. M. Staw (eds.), *Research in Organizational Behavior* 7 (1985): 171–226.

Weill, Peter, and Jeanne Ross. *IT Governance: How Top Performers Manage IT Decision Rights for Superior Results.* Boston, Mass.: Harvard Business School Press, 2004.

Wernerfelt, B. "A Resource-Based View of the Firm." *Strategic Management Journal* 5:2 (1984): 171–180.

Wreden, N. "Executive Champions: The Vital Link Between Strategy Formulation and Implementation." *Harvard Management Update* 7:9 (2002): 3–5.

Wynne, Joe. *Running with Change.* August 2006, Gantthead.com.

Young, M., and J. E. Post. "Managing to Communicate, Communicating to Manage," *Organizational Dynamics,* Summer (1993): 31–43.

Zarella, Egidio, Mark Tims, Bill Carr, and Walter Palk. "Global IT Project Management Survey" (KPMG Advisory). Montvale, N.J.: KPMG International, 2005.

Index

About the Authors

Lia Tjahjana has more than seven years of project management experience in various industries, including finance and construction, both in the public and private sectors. An entrepreneur, she also has had experience with establishing and running an online business. She has a master of liberal arts in management from Harvard University, and a master of engineering science in project management and a bachelor of civil engineering from the University of New South Wales in Sydney.

Paul Dwyer, PMP has been involved in project management in the financial services industry for over ten years. He has worked for many Fortune 500 companies, implementing high-profile information technology projects across multiple organizations, both on- and offshore. A senior development manager for a leading U.S. financial institution, Paul is also president of the Ireland Chamber of Commerce United States, New England Chapter, a trade organization based in Boston, and he runs their small business incubator center in the city's financial district. Paul holds a degree in computing science from the University of Ulster and is a certified Project Management Professional.

Mohsin Habib is associate professor of management at the University of Massachusetts–Boston. He received his PhD in strategic management from the University of North Carolina, Chapel Hill. He teaches strategy and international management at the University of Massachusetts and the Harvard University Extension School. He has been involved with executive education seminars on strategy for management groups in the United States and abroad. His current research interest focuses on strategy, competition, and sustainable development, especially for developing markets. He has presented his findings in numerous conferences and has been published in reputed journals, including the *Strategic Management Journal, Journal of International Business Studies*, and *Entrepreneurship Theory and Practice.*